SHAKESPEARE PROBLEMS

Edited by A. W. POLLARD & J. DOVER WILSON

V. A STUDY OF
LOVE'S LABOUR'S LOST

A STUDY OF
LOVE'S LABOUR'S LOST

BY

FRANCES A. YATES

CAMBRIDGE
AT THE UNIVERSITY PRESS
1936

CAMBRIDGE UNIVERSITY PRESS
Cambridge, New York, Melbourne, Madrid, Cape Town,
Singapore, São Paulo, Delhi, Mexico City

Cambridge University Press
The Edinburgh Building, Cambridge CB2 8RU, UK

Published in the United States of America by Cambridge University Press, New York

www.cambridge.org
Information on this title: www.cambridge.org/9781107695986

First published 1936
First paperback edition 2013

A catalogue record for this publication is available from the British Library

ISBN 978-1-107-69598-6 Paperback

CONTENTS

APPENDICES

PREFACE

When Shakespeare introduced the character of Holofernes, the pedant, into his topical comedy of *Love's Labour's Lost*, did he or did he not intend him as a satirical portrait of John Florio? This is a question which has often been asked and which a student of Florio's life and works must eventually face. I had originally intended to devote a chapter to it at the end of my life of Florio; but that project was soon abandoned because there proved to be far more material for the biography than I had imagined, and, as I came to know more about Florio, I realised that the Holofernes problem would require a book to itself. By kind permission of the editors, the resulting volume forms one of the Shakespeare Problems Series.

The answer to the question "Is Holofernes Florio?" turns out to be "Yes and no"; and in the course of reaching this answer we find that Florio has introduced us to people who can explain, not merely his own part in the play, but very nearly the whole secret of the topical application of *Love's Labour's Lost*. The elucidation of a few jokes about comic schoolmasters leads on to matters of much greater importance, matters indeed upon which I should never have had the temerity to embark had they not turned out to be concealed in the problem which I had set myself.

The present study does not by any means exhaust the possibilities of the material upon which it is based, and the student will notice many points at which further work is waiting to be done. I do not expect, nor wish, that any of my findings should be accepted without cautious testing of the evidence.

I should like to express my grateful thanks to Dr A. W. Pollard for his most valuable suggestions as to the arrangement of my material, and other helpful criticisms which have been of the greatest assistance and encouragement to me.

FRANCES A. YATES

Christmas 1935

INTRODUCTION

I. THE TEXT

Love's Labour's Lost is one of those plays which was published in Quarto during Shakespeare's lifetime. There are thus two original printed texts, the Quarto published in 1598 and the Folio published in 1623 in the first collected edition of Shakespeare's plays. Modern bibliographical research is demonstrating that a text such as the "good" 1598 Quarto of *Love's Labour's Lost* is more than likely to have been printed from Shakespeare's autograph manuscript. Professor Dover Wilson bases his edition of the play in the Cambridge *New Shakespeare* primarily upon the 1598 Quarto text, and it is from that remarkable edition that quotations are made throughout this book. But the modern editor does not ignore the Folio text, for although *Love's Labour's Lost* in the Folio was printed from a copy of the Quarto, it contains alterations and additions derived from some other source. The character of these alterations suggests that this other source was the prompt-book used in the theatre when the play was being performed.[1]

On the title-page of this 1598 Quarto which is the primary source of the text are the words "Newly corrected and augmented". These words, and various other bibliographical considerations, led Dr Pollard to think it highly probable that an earlier pirated edition of the play, a "bad" Quarto, had preceded the 1598 Quarto, although no copy of this has yet come to light.[2] Some experts, notably Professor Dover Wilson, think that the words "newly cor-

---

[1] *Love's Labour's Lost* in the Cambridge *New Shakespeare*, edited by Sir A. Quiller-Couch and J. Dover Wilson, 1923, pp. 98, 186–91.
[2] A. W. Pollard, *Shakespeare's Fight with the Pirates*, Shakespeare Problems Series, 1920, p. 47.

rected and augmented", in addition to hinting at the preceding "bad" Quarto, also mean that Shakespeare had revised and altered the manuscript of the play, that he had written a version of it some years before and that this early version was later touched up by his hand. According to them the "newly corrected and augmented" 1598 Quarto was printed from this revised manuscript and they claim to be able to see many evidences in the printed text of the points at which the revision was made. But Sir Edmund Chambers[1] and others think that the existence of a previous pirated edition of the play would fully account for the words on the 1598 title-page and they do not think that there is sufficient evidence for the theory of extensive revision by Shakespeare of a first draft of the play.

The present study is entirely concerned with the working out of the topical bearing of the play and only touches upon textual or bibliographical problems in so far as these affect, or are affected by, the question of the date. The allusions to events and people which I believe that I can trace lead me to agree with Sir Edmund Chambers in thinking that the play was written practically as we have it (although some dangerous matters may possibly have been toned down before printing) some time during the year 1595. At the same time I am aware that the revision problem introduces a certain degree of hesitation into the dating of the composition of the play from allusions.

II. THE LITERARY HISTORY OF THE PLAY

Everyone is agreed that *Love's Labour's Lost* is one of the most topical of all Shakespeare's plays, that it bristles throughout with allusions to contemporary events and to living persons, and innumerable are the efforts which have been made to explain its meaning in terms of the dramatist's environment. In the following brief sketch of the literary

---

[1] Sir E. Chambers, *William Shakespeare*, I, 333–5.

history of the play I cannot hope to mention every suggestion which has ever been brought forward in connection with it but only to outline those theories which stand with some stability amidst the general welter of surmise.

A topical problem confronts us before the play has even begun, for at the head of the list of *dramatis personae* we read the following four names: "Ferdinand, *King of Navarre*; Berowne, Longaville, Dumaine, *young lords, attending on the King.*" It was Sir Sidney Lee who first pointed out[1] that these were names which would be in everybody's mouth during the fifteen-nineties because they were those of famous leaders in the contemporary French civil wars. But the real King of Navarre's name was, of course, Henry and not Ferdinand, whilst the Duc de Mayenne (Dumaine), far from being a young lord attendant upon him, was one of the heads of the Guise faction and therefore his sworn enemy. So that if Shakespeare intended these names to represent contemporary French history he carried out his intention in a singularly muddle-headed, or else wilfully frivolous, manner. Moreover, there is very little real history in the story of the play and most of what there is appears to be derived, as Professor Abel Lefranc showed, from certain episodes which occurred round about the year 1578 and which are mentioned in the *Mémoires* of Marguerite de Valois.[2] As these *Mémoires* and other accounts of Henry of Navarre and Marguerite de Valois were not yet available in print, Sir Edmund Chambers thinks that Shakespeare must have obtained any real historical information he deigned to use in the play from "some English or French traveller".[3] So much for the light-hearted use of a topical "news from France" atmosphere in this comedy.

[1] In the *Gentleman's Magazine*, October 1880, pp. 447–58.
[2] Abel Lefranc, *Sous le masque de "William Shakespeare"*, 1919, II, 33–103.
[3] *Op. cit.* I, 338.

It is generally admitted that echoes of the famous controversy between Gabriel Harvey and Thomas Nashe are to be discerned in *Love's Labour's Lost*. Numerous parallels between remarks in the play and passages in the pamphlets have been collected[1] and although not all of these are accepted by all critics, there is one which seems conclusive, even to Professor H. B. Charlton[2] who seeks to minimise the Harvey-Nashe influence in the play. Alluding to Nashe's *Pierce Penilesse* (1592) Harvey says in his *Pierces Supererogation* (1593):

> She knew what she said, that intituled Pierce, the hoggeshead of witt: Penniles, the tospot of eloquence: & Nashe, the verye inuentor of Asses. She it is, that must broach the barrell of thy frisking conceite, and canonise the Patriarke of newe writers.[3]

This is compared with,

> *Holofernes.* Master Person—quasi pierce-one? And if one
> should be pierced, which is the one?
> *Costard.*   Marry, master schoolmaster, he that is likeliest to
> a hogshead.[4]

There is no doubt that Harvey and Nashe lurk behind these lines, for the play on "pierce" and "person" proves this. Harvey's *Pierces Supererogation* was a reply to Nashe's *Pierce Penilesse*, and since "pierce" was then pronounced "perce", as Chaucer spelt it, Shakespeare's pun on "pierce" and "person" unmistakably refers to Nashe and to his quarrel with Harvey. There are other passages which bear this out. As the *New Shakespeare* editors say "Puns upon 'purse', 'pen', 'penny' obtrude themselves throughout the play when Moth is assailed or retorts: all of them meaning-

---

[1] See particularly H. C. Hart's edition of *Love's Labour's Lost* in the *Arden Shakespeare*.

[2] H. B. Charlton, "The Date of *Love's Labour's Lost*", *Modern Language Review*, XIII, 1918, pp. 257-66, 387-400.

[3] Gabriel Harvey, *Works*, ed. A. B. Grosart, 1884, II, 91.

[4] IV. ii. 87-90.

less (so far as we can discover) unless referable to Nashe's *Pierce (i.q. Purse) Penilesse.*"[1] Armado calls Moth his "tender Juvenal", and "young Juvenal" seems to have been Nashe's nickname among his contemporaries. The style of Moth's longest speech is reminiscent of Nashe's style and this, together with other details which they point out,[2] has led the *New Shakespeare* editors to the conclusion that Moth, in all probability, was meant to represent Thomas Nashe. The suggestion that Moth is Nashe was also made by Fleay who sought to connect the play with the Martin Marprelate controversy and to identify Armado, Holofernes, Costard and the other members of the comic underplot with the anti-Martinist writers Lyly, Nashe, Kempe, Bishop Cooper and Anthony Munday.[3] But the Marprelate controversy had faded into the Harvey-Nashe dispute by the time that *Love's Labour's Lost* was written and thus, although Fleay was probably right about Nashe, his other suggested "originals" may be abandoned. The most recent enthusiast for the Harvey-Nashe influence in the play is Mr Rupert Taylor who believes that he can find traces in it of Nashe's *Have With You to Saffron Walden* (1596).[4]

One of the most interesting of the already existing theories seeking to explain the topicalities of *Love's Labour's Lost* is that which maintains that the bulk of the satire in the play was directed at Sir Walter Raleigh and his group of mathematicians, astronomers, and poets. It was the late Arthur Acheson,[5] following a clue of Professor Minto's, who first suggested that there may be a connection between

---

[1] *Love's Labour's Lost*, in the Cambridge *New Shakespeare* edition, Introduction, p. xxii.

[2] *Ibid.* pp. xx–xxiii.

[3] F. G. Fleay, "Shakespeare and Puritanism", *Anglia*, 1884, VII, pp. 223–31.

[4] Rupert Taylor, *The Date of "Love's Labour's Lost"*, 1932, pp. 34–51.

[5] Arthur Acheson, *Shakespeare and the Rival Poet*, 1903.

Chapman's *Shadow of Night* (1594) and *Love's Labour's Lost.*

> O paradox! Black is the badge of hell,
> The hue of dungeons and the School of Night...[1]

exclaims Navarre, and it is believed that Raleigh's coterie was known as the "School of Night", that Chapman's *Shadow of Night* emanated from that coterie, and that when Shakespeare makes Navarre speak of a "School of Night" in the play, this was a topical allusion which would have been as clear as day to the audience. It is further noted that in the lines,

> Beauty is bought by judgement of the eye,
> Not uttred by base sale of *chapmen's* tongues,[2]

Shakespeare may be alluding to Chapman's surname.

The "School of Night" theory is most interestingly set forth by the *New Shakespeare* editors in their introduction to *Love's Labour's Lost.* When Navarre and his attendant lords, Berowne, Dumaine and Longaville, determine to spend three years in seclusion and the pursuit of knowledge it is clear that astronomy is one of the subjects which they intend to study. Berowne obviously has scientific observers of the heavens in mind when he says:

> These earthly godfathers of heaven's lights,
>   That give a name to every fixéd star,
> Have no more profit of their shining nights,
>   Than those that walk and wot not what they are.[3]

The play bristles with continual hinting references to darkness, light, day, night, the sun, the moon, the stars— even to mathematical calculations. The *New Shakespeare* editors make the interesting observation that "none of the fantastics in this play can count". They give examples to illustrate this statement. "Holofernes shares with the other 'worthies' a curious incompetence in arithmetic: they can-

---

[1] IV. iii. 250–1.   [2] II. i. 15–16.   [3] I. i. 88–91.

not tell their own number when they get together. Armado
(I. ii. 39–54) cannot multiply one by three; Costard (v. ii.
488 *et seq.*) cannot multiply three by three. 'I am ill at
reck'ning, it fitteth the spirit of a tapster', explains Armado,
and Costard groans, 'O Lord, sir, it were a pity you should
get your living by reck'ning, sir.' Again, in III. i. 87–97,
we can see Armado reckoning up three laboriously on
his fingers until Moth 'stays the odds by adding four'.
That these passages play insistently on *somebody's* mathematical pretensions (well known to the audience) is surely
evident."[1]

Raleigh was the political rival of the Essex-Southampton
faction and since many things seem to point towards Shakespeare's sympathies having been strongly engaged on the
Essex-Southampton side it would be not unnatural to find
him making fun of Raleigh and his friends. The allusions
to heaven's lights, to mathematical calculations, to a "School
of Night"—indeed the whole pretentious plan with which
Navarre sets out of making his court a "little academe"—
are therefore to be explained, according to this theory, as
a mocking attack on the pretensions of the learned Raleigh
group, one of the main interests of which was the study
of the new Copernican astronomy. Raleigh himself is
thought to be touched by the satire and also his familiar
spirit Thomas Hariot, whose studies in optics and refraction are thought by some[2] to have something to do with
the continual punning in the play on words such as "light",
"eyes", "eyesight", "see", "look", and so on.

An important feature of the "School of Night" theory
is the use it makes of George Chapman and his works.
Chapman seems to have been poet-in-chief to the Raleigh

[1] *Love's Labour's Lost*, ed. *cit*. Introduction, p. xxxi note.
[2] Miss Ethel Seaton made some interesting points in this connection
in a paper on Hariot which she read to the Elizabethan Literary
Society in February 1933. See also Dr G. B. Harrison's *Elizabethan
Journal*, 1928, pp. 398–400.

group. His poetry has a strong intellectual, or, as the Elizabethan would say, "artistic" bent. He delights in a darkness, a profundity, which is not addressed to vulgar ears but to those choice and learned spirits who are capable of interpreting it. For him, learning is

> the soul's actual frame,
> Without which 'tis a blank, a smoke-hid flame. . . .[1]

He published in 1594 an extremely obscure poem called *The Shadow of Night* which extols night and darkness in curious terms.

> Since Night brings terror to our frailties still,
> And shameless Day doth marble us in ill;
> All you possessed with indepresséd spirits,
> Endued with nimble and aspiring wits,
> Come consecrate with me to sacred Night
> Your whole endeavours, and detest the light.
> Sweet Peace's richest crown is made of stars,
> Most certain guides of honoured mariners,
> No pen can anything eternal write
> That is not steeped in humour of the Night.

Embedded in all this mystery are hints which seem to suggest that Chapman was interested in the new astronomical investigations and was not insensible to the poetry of higher mathematics. "Night" with him appears to typify the contemplation of deep matters, of those things hid and barred from common sense the knowledge of which is study's godlike recompense. Thus, when he says that no pen can anything eternal write that is not steeped in humour of the Night, he appears to mean that much learning and a rigid intellectual training are an essential preparation for the development of a poet's powers. It was to this kind of argument, it is said, that Shakespeare intended his *Love's Labour's Lost*, with its mockery of high-

[1] *The Tears of Peace*, 1609.

flown intellectual pretensions and its allusion to the "School of Night", as a reply.

I think one may say that this theory is now more or less generally accepted. The studious young men in the play can be interpreted as representing either the Raleigh group, immersed in their studies, or the Essex-Southampton group who laugh at schemes of that kind. Chapman lets us know who some of Raleigh's friends were in his dedication to the *Shadow of Night* where he mentions the Earl of Derby (known as Lord Strange before coming into the title), Lord Hunsdon, and the Earl of Northumberland as being amongst those who pursue knowledge with proper seriousness. Efforts have been made to connect Derby with the King of Navarre in the play through his Christian name, which was Ferdinand, and through some punning on the word "strange".[1] Lord Strange became Earl of Derby and also King of Man (the Isle of Man) in 1593 and died in the following year. No one, so far as I know, has attempted to look particularly for the other two mentioned by Chapman, namely Hunsdon and Northumberland, among the young lords in the comedy. If one takes the view that Berowne and his friends in their revolt against undue book-learning represent rather the lively Essex and his followers, then his two intimates the earls of Southampton and Rutland suggest themselves for inclusion.[2] In either case the play becomes an expression of the spirit of aristocratic faction.

Besides the joke against the members of the "School of Night" there was also afoot in the circle for which *Love's Labour's Lost* was written a joke against schoolmasters and pedants. Holofernes was a schoolmaster, constantly quoting

---

[1] Janet Spens, "Notes on *Love's Labour's Lost*", *Review of English Studies*, VII, July 1931, pp. 331–4.

[2] J. Dover Wilson, *The Essential Shakespeare*, 1932, pp. 65–6. Professor Dover Wilson associates Derby with Essex, Southampton and Rutland.

pedantic tags in Latin or in modern languages. He kept
a most mysterious school, or "charge-house".

> *Armado.*   Arts-man, preambulate. We will be singled from
> the barbarous.. . .Do you not educate youth at the
> charge-house on the top of the mountain?
> *Holofernes.* Or mons, the hill.
> *Armado.*   At your sweet pleasure, for the mountain.
> *Holofernes.* I do, sans question.[1]

"What was this charge-house? and where was this mountain?" enquire the *New Shakespeare* editors. "We are not
told. The words refer to nothing that goes before or that
follows, or indeed to anything else in the play. Yet they
are pointed enough. The skirmish of the two fantastics
over 'mountain' and 'mons' clearly underscores some
point that the audience would take. It is lost to us: but
can there be any doubt that Armado and Holofernes have
stepped out of the fable for a moment to exchange a sentence
or two of topical 'back-chat'?"[2]

Some of the dialogue between the pedants and the fantastics seems to be a kind of satire on the textbooks generally
read in schools, such as the eclogues of Mantuan, from
which Holofernes misquotes the first line, or the numerous
Latin dialogues or "colloquies" which were designed to
teach boys to speak Latin. Professor Dover Wilson points
out that in their second scene Holofernes and Sir Nathaniel
"are made to parody the Latin colloquies which formed
part of the staple fare in grammar schools of the period".[3]

> *Sir Nathaniel.* Laus Deo, bone intelligo.
> *Holofernes.*   Bone?—bon fort bon!—Priscian a little
> scratched—'twill serve.
> *Sir Nathaniel.* Videsne quis venit?
> *Holofernes.*   Video, et gaudeo.[4]

---

[1] v. i. 77–83.
[2] *Love's Labour's Lost, ed. cit.* Introduction, pp. xviii–xix.
[3] J. Dover Wilson, "The Schoolmaster in Shakespeare's Plays",
in *Essays by Divers Hands being. . .Transactions of the Royal Society
of Literature*, IX, 1930, p. 30.   [4] v. i. 27–31.

Evidently a part of the laughter of the play was aimed either at schoolmasters and their textbooks in general or at some particular teacher or teachers.

Pedantic affectation is only one of the many kinds of affectation at which Shakespeare is glancing a malicious eye. He parodies the various literary crazes of the day— euphuism, arcadianism, Gongorism, Guevarism, Petrarchism and the sonneteering fashion, the mania for proverbs and for strange Latinate words.[1] And again the question arises whether this mockery was a general satire on the age or whether he had in view any individuals who were particularly remarkable for precious writing or for fantastic speech.

Attention has more recently been drawn[2] to the fact that at the Gray's Inn Revels of 1594–5, in the course of which Shakespeare's *Comedy of Errors* was performed, some use was made of Russian disguise. It is thought that this may have influenced the Russian masque in *Love's Labour's Lost*, and there are other curious correspondences between this play and *Gesta Grayorum* which await further examination.

These applications of the play to contemporary life are all now more or less generally accepted (with the possible exception of the last) as containing at any rate some degree of truth. But when one attempts to go further and to pin down this or that character as a "portrait" of a contemporary one finds oneself in the thick of a most bewildering array of conjectural candidates. Some have taken the "French news" names quite literally as portraits of Henry of Navarre, the Maréchal Biron, the Duc de Longueville and the Duc de Mayenne. Others, as has

[1] This subject is interestingly treated in a paper by G. D. Willcock on *Shakespeare as a Critic of Language*, published for the Shakespeare Association, 1934.

[2] By Sir Edmund Chambers (*op. cit.* I, 335–6) and, independently, by Rupert Taylor (*op. cit.* pp. 1–20).

already been said, see in these four young men reflections
(not portraits) of the members of the Raleigh or of the
Essex groups. Some Italian critics have thought that they
could detect resemblances between Berowne and the Italian
philosopher Giordano Bruno who spent about two years
in England from 1583 onwards.[1] A suggestion, now
entirely forgotten, was made in 1872[2] to the effect that
the "original" of Rosaline might be Lady Penelope Rich,
the heroine of Sidney's sonnets, and when one remembers
that Lady Rich was Essex's sister this is an idea which has
something to commend it.

For the comic characters, and particularly for those chief
butts of the play's wit, Holofernes and Armado, there is a
still larger array of possible "originals". Those chiefly
interested in the echoes of the Harvey-Nashe controversy
in Shakespeare have chosen Armado, and sometimes Holofernes, as a portrait of the pedantic Gabriel Harvey. When
the "School of Night" interpretation receives the greatest
stress, the over-intellectual Chapman becomes Armado, or
Holofernes,[3] unless Raleigh himself is Armado and Holofernes is the mathematician, Thomas Hariot, who was his
close associate.

Then again, Holofernes was a schoolmaster and so one
is free to look round for likely pedagogic "originals",
hitting perhaps on Richard Mulcaster, or on Thomas
Hunt, who might have taught Shakespeare at Stratford-
on-Avon grammar school. But if the Earl of Derby wrote
the play, and not Shakespeare at all, then Holofernes
naturally becomes Derby's tutor, one Richard Lloyd. On
the other hand, the Earl of Oxford as author would seem
to favour Harvey as Holofernes. One must not forget in
the excitement of looking for schoolmasters that both

[1] Benedetto Croce, *Nuove curiosità storiche*, 1922, pp. 121–2.
[2] Gerald Massey, *The Secret Drama of Shakspere's Sonnets*, 1872.
[3] Arthur Acheson, *Shakespeare and the Rival Poet*, 1903; J. M.
Robertson, *Shakespeare and Chapman*, 1917.

Armado and Holofernes use exaggerated and fantastic language. This opens up at once an enormous, indeed practically unlimited, choice of "originals". The most obvious name to mention here is that of John Lyly who used to be much quoted in connection with this play, and another suggestion is Antonio Perez, an eccentric Spaniard who amused Essex and his friends considerably and whose letters certainly are very much in Armado's vein.[1]

Last but not least comes the celebrated Italian teacher, John Florio. Or rather he is not last but first, for to Florio belongs the distinction of being the original "original" of Holofernes. In 1747 William Warburton made the following observation:

> *Enter*—Holofernes,] There is very little personal reflexion in *Shakespear*. Either the virtue of those times, or the candour of our author, has so effected, that his satire is, for the most part, general, and as himself says,
>
> > ...*his taxing like a wild goose flies,*
> > *Unclaim'd of any man....*
>
> The place before us seems to be an exception. For by *Holofernes* is designed a particular character, a pedant and schoolmaster of our author's time, one *John Florio*, a teacher of the *Italian* tongue in *London*, who has given us a small dictionary of that language under the title of *A world of words*....[2]

Thus calmly did the high-handed Warburton initiate the great Holofernes hunt, and he believed further that Florio replied to Shakespeare's attack on him in the long and extremely abusive address to the reader which he inserted in the 1598 edition of his dictionary which contains the phrase:

> *Let* Aristophanes *and his comedians make plaies, and scowre their mouthes on* Socrates; *those very mouthes they make to vilifie, shall be the meanes to amplifie his vertue.*

[1] Martin Hume, *Spanish Influence on English Literature*, 1905, pp. 258–74.
[2] *The Works of Shakespear...collated...corrected and emended... by Mr Pope and Mr Warburton*, 1747, vol. II, pp. 227–8.

"Here", says Warburton, "*Shakespear* is so plainly marked out as not to be mistaken."

There are two points to notice about this Warburton theory. In the first place it has a kind of prestige as an "antique". Warburton wrote his note on Holofernes and Florio one hundred and thirty-one years after the death of Shakespeare. It is a long time, but not such a long time as the considerably more than three centuries which now divide us from him. I am rather struck by the way in which Warburton describes Florio. A teacher of Italian in London, he calls him, and the author of a dictionary. Such exactly was the kind of memory of Florio which lingered on when his translation of Montaigne and his many other activities were forgotten. The last mention of him which I have been able to trace, before he disappeared into the oblivion from which he was not rescued until 1885, is the notice which Torriano printed in 1673 in his grammar called *Italian Reviv'd*. Torriano, an Italian teacher, gave in this book the address at which possible pupils might find him. He is teaching, he says,

At the Sign of Resolute *John Florio*, Author, of the *Italian Dictionary*, in *Miter Court* in Fleet-street, over against *Fetter Lane*.[1]

1673 to 1747 is seventy-four years, not too long a time, perhaps, for some tradition anent Florio and Shakespeare to have lingered for Warburton to pick up and fix in this very positive note of his. To state with such confidence that Holofernes was Florio seems an extraordinary assertion for anyone, even an eighteenth-century editor, to have made entirely out of his imagination. Secondly, Warburton has been much abused for having "obscured" the fact that Florio's anger in his dictionary preface is directed at a person whose initials are "H. S." and who therefore can-

---

[1] See my *John Florio, the Life of an Italian in Shakespeare's England*, 1934, p. 326.

not be Shakespeare.[1] But Warburton had seen something which neither Furness nor anyone else has troubled to make clear but which is perfectly obvious when Florio's address to the reader is studied attentively, namely that the Italian is attacking not one but several enemies.[2] One of these enemies had the initials "H. S." (and was, as we now know, Hugh Sanford, secretary to the Earl of Pembroke[3]) but the initials of the other enemies are not given and may therefore be filled in from the imagination.

Nevertheless, in the bald form entirely unsupported by evidence in which Warburton originally promulgated it, the theory of Florio as the "original" of Holofernes is certainly not convincing. Dr Johnson soon threw cold water upon it and so did many subsequent eighteenth- and nineteenth-century editors and critics.[4] Malone objected to it on the grounds that the Earl of Southampton was the patron of both Florio and Shakespeare and that the latter would therefore have been very unlikely to hold Florio up to ridicule. This seems on the surface a good argument and it has been constantly repeated. Yet one might say that in the earlier days of Shakespearean criticism the majority supported Warburton's opinion. Farmer pointed out that Florio had criticised the English drama, saying that the plays acted in England were "neither right comedies, nor right tragedies" but "representations of histories, without any decorum". This, he thought, might have annoyed Shakespeare. Steevens also supported the identification of Florio with Holofernes. Hunter disapproved of it on the whole but introduced a new element into the problem by suggesting that there might be touches

---

[1] H. H. Furness, *New Variorum Edition of Shakespeare*, XIV, *Loues Labour's Lost*, 1904, pp. 351–2.

[2] *John Florio*, pp. 192–4.   [3] *Ibid.* pp. 194–209.

[4] See Furness, *ed. cit.* pp. 351–7, for a summary of all the opinions on this subject.

of Florio in Armado. He quoted the following conversation between Armado and Jaquenetta:

> *Jaquenetta.* Lord, how wise you are!
> *Armado.*　　 I will tell thee wonders.
> *Jaquenetta.* With that face?[1]

This he compared to Sir William Cornwallis's description of Florio, "a fellow less beholding to nature for his fortunes than wit, yet lesser for his face than his fortune", and suggested that there was perhaps something peculiar about Florio's face. "With that face" was a common cant phrase and its presence here proves nothing whatever, although the expression does as a matter of fact occur in one of Florio's manuals:

> What should Nature haue made of thee with that face?[2]

But as time went on Florio was gradually ousted from his proud position as the sole possible original of Holofernes or Armado by the crowds of new pretenders to the honour, and, what with all this competition on the one hand, and on the other hand the growth of the conception of an Olympian Shakespeare towering in solitary greatness aloof and apart from all his mundane surroundings, Warburton's identification of Holofernes with Florio sank very low indeed in the general estimation and came to be seldom mentioned, or only mentioned with a sneer. Arthur Acheson attempted to remedy this state of affairs in 1920 by proving, but only to his own satisfaction, that Armado is Florio.[3] The Countess de Chambrun[4] next revived Florio as the original of Holofernes, supporting her arguments by a good deal of quotation from his *First Fruits* and *Second Fruits*. Like almost everyone else who has

---

[1] I. ii. 132–4.　　　　　　　[2] *Second Fruits*, Sig. S 3.
[3] Arthur Acheson, *Shakespeare's Lost Years in London* 1586–1592, 1920.
[4] Clara Longworth de Chambrun, *Giovanni Florio*, 1921; *Shakespeare Actor-Poet*, 1927.

examined these two extremely rare books with any care—many of those who have theorised in the past about Florio and Shakespeare have obviously never opened them—she felt convinced that they were of great importance to the student of Shakespeare and she did valuable service in insisting upon their significance. But she persisted in maintaining, as Acheson had done, that the "H. S." whom Florio attacked in his dictionary preface was Shakespeare, a position which was never strong owing to the difficulty of explaining why Florio did not say "W. S." if he meant William Shakespeare, and which is now quite untenable as "H. S." has been proved to be Hugh Sanford. On the whole one may say that the presence of Florio in *Love's Labour's Lost* is now regarded as a possibility for which there is no really conclusive evidence but which cannot be entirely dismissed with Olympian scorn.

We have not yet done with Holofernes and Armado because they also possess an extensive literary ancestry. It is undoubtedly an important and significant fact that the pedant in Rabelais bears the same name as the pedant in this play, and Malone believed that Holofernes is a compound of the two characters Thubal Holoferne and Janotus de Bragmardo created by the great French humorist. Others besides Dr Johnson have noted resemblances between the speech of Holofernes and that of the pedant called Rombus in Sir Philip Sidney's masque *The Lady of May*. Shakespeare may have heard of the Latin play *Pædantius*, in which Harvey was satirised, and he was almost certainly familiar with the comedies of Lyly in one of which, *Endymion*, there is a braggart called Sir Tophas and his page who remind one of Armado and Moth. Some of these resemblances, however, might go back to some knowledge of Latin comedy, of Plautus or of Terence, which Shakespeare had in common with other writers of his day.

Much the most important of the influences of this kind

which may have had a bearing upon the formation of the comic characters in *Love's Labour's Lost* is that of the *commedia dell' arte*, the popular comedy played by the troupes of Italian comedians who wandered all over Europe. As is well known, the Italians used certain set types of character, or "masks", upon which they based their improvisations. No one can read Miss K. M. Lea's analyses[1] of the masks of the Pedant and of the Spanish Braggart or "capitano" without realising that here was the rough outline from which Shakespeare's pedant and braggart were constructed. In some of the speech-headings in the text Holofernes and Armado are actually referred to as "Ped." and "Brag." instead of by their names. Mr O. J. Campbell has worked out in some detail the traces of *commedia dell' arte* influence in *Love's Labour's Lost* in an essay[2] which is one of the most valuable pieces of work on the play which have appeared since the *New Shakespeare* edition. We understand now that the brags and high-flown hyperbole of Armado, the proverbs, synonyms, strange words, Latin and foreign tags which fall from the lips of Holofernes, place them at once as two types of character which were familiar figures on every stage in Europe.

Yet, as Sir Edmund Chambers says, the fact that "the underworld of *Love's Labour's Lost* represents the stock masks of Italian comedy" does not do away with the possibility that there may be "personal touches in the reproduction of them", although it is an exaggeration to speak of "portraits".[3] Under cover of the Pedant and the Braggart Shakespeare did indeed glance maliciously now and then towards certain living pedants and braggarts who were well known to himself and his audience, and the

[1] K. M. Lea, *Italian Popular Comedy*, 1934, I, pp. 39–50.
[2] O. J. Campbell, "*Love's Labour's Lost* Re-studied", in *Studies in Shakespeare, Milton and Donne*, by Members of the English department of the University of Michigan, 1925, pp. 3–45.
[3] *Op. cit.* I, 336.

"originals", so long as they are not allowed to get out of hand, may help us to find out who these people were. One must never forget to reckon with the subtlety of Shakespeare and with the fact that he was intensely creative. The imaginative artist uses but does not exactly reproduce his experience. Holofernes may be a stock pedant, he may be stuffed with traits reminiscent of people whom Shakespeare knew, but he is also Holofernes himself, a new creature with a life and a will of his own, and no original-hunter can pin him down as a "portrait" of this or of that person. As Professor Dover Wilson has said: "Shakespeare was a dramatic artist not a journalist, and above all he was subtle. He hardly ever goes out of his way to make a topical hit; he glances at the business in passing, obliquely and in hints, rather than by overt reference."[1]

The position as it stands to-day is therefore that *Love's Labour's Lost* is an intensely topical play which glances at current events in France, at the Harvey-Nashe controversy, at Raleigh and his group of scientists, astronomers and poets, and at all kinds of schoolmasterly and precious affectations, the satire being worked in with subtlety and without resorting to crude portraiture. Yet the play remains a problem. Many things are still entirely unexplained, the "charge-house" school for instance, and what was the connection between the stars of the astronomers and the eyes of ladies. There are not only serious gaps in our knowledge of the scope of the play's satire, there is incoherence and confusion amongst what we do know. Why should Harvey and Nashe be mixed up with the members of the "School of Night" and what do schoolmasters know about stars? This book is an attempt to provide an answer to these and other questions.

---

[1] *The Essential Shakespeare*, p. 13.

III. THE PRESENT ARGUMENT

I propose now to hand the reader a kind of outline of the answer to the problem of *Love's Labour's Lost* which I am about to advance. Having a rough idea of the object and general direction of the journey he will then, I hope, be encouraged to follow me with some degree of patience along rather strange and devious paths.

This is not an attempt to provide a set of contemporary "originals" for the characters in the play. I entirely agree that Shakespeare as a topical dramatist is always indirect and subtle, never obvious and crude. Moreover, I believe in the Italianate origin of the "types" to which the comic characters belong and, further, that the whole grouping of the main characters in symmetrical groups of four and the artificial development of the action of the play is also probably derived from some Italian plot. In short, Shakespeare is using in this play a kind of rough scaffolding, both of the plot and of the characters, which he took ready-made from somewhere.

Into this mould he poured his topical satire. I believe that from behind the mask of Holofernes, the Pedant, Shakespeare glanced his darts at, not one, but several living people, and that the same is true of many of the other characters. Some of these malicious glances can be traced to the persons who provoked them, but from that it does not follow that these persons are the "originals" of the characters but merely that they are a part of the composite topical background of the play. Such is the attitude adopted in this book as to Shakespeare's methods of using topical satire, and it is upon these general premises that the particular arguments are based. These arguments run, in outline, as follows.

I begin where Warburton began, with Florio. First of all the traditional objection to the possibility of the presence of satire on Florio in the play, on the ground that the Earl of Southampton was both Shakespeare's and Florio's patron, is shown to be unsound. Southampton was a Catholic and a minor when Florio, a Protestant, was appointed as his language-tutor by his Protestant guardian, Lord Burleigh, perhaps in succession to the Catholic Swithin Wells. Southampton might therefore have had political and personal reasons for disliking Florio, although the latter was ostensibly in his "paie and patronage". Then some other evidence from our new knowledge of Florio's life and circumstances is brought forward. The most important of this is the fact that in 1593 John Eliot published a book of French-English dialogues called *Ortho-epia Gallica* which is an attack on Florio, and others, and a parody of his two books of Italian-English dialogues. There was thus a joke against Florio in the air and it was "topical" to laugh at him. This, in itself, immediately strengthens the case for the presence of satire on Florio in *Love's Labour's Lost*. And when, further, it is discovered that there are certain resemblances between some of Eliot's jokes against Florio and some of the jokes in the play which tradition has thought to be directed against him, that case is practically established. Although it is an over-statement to say that Florio, or anyone else, is the "original" of Holofernes or of any other character, it is, in my opinion, undoubtedly true that he is one of the people against whom the oblique satire of the play is directed.

The pursuit of Florio leads the argument to Eliot, of whose parody of Florio Shakespeare seems to have knowledge. Eliot's *Ortho-epia Gallica* is next shown, by quotation from other plays, to be a book which was certainly known to Shakespeare. Satire on Florio is only a part of the scope of Eliot's dialogues which are a Rabelaisian parody of Latin school textbooks and of the modern-language textbooks of refugee language-teachers in general —not only those of Florio—conceived rather in the anti-alien spirit of those years. Parallels between all this and the traces of Rabelais and of satire on textbooks in *Love's Labour's Lost* are drawn which suggest that *Ortho-epia Gallica* is the clue, not only to the presence of Florio in the play, but to its whole anti-pedagogic trend. The "charge-house" school may be one of the new type of private school kept in the City of London by the French Protestant refugee schoolmasters against whom Eliot inveighs, and the taunt which Eliot hurls at the refugee Frenchmen—that they care nothing for the wars and miseries in their own unhappy country so long as they can live comfortably in England—may have something to do with the "French news" names in *Love's Labour's Lost*.

These Eliot-Florio clues lead on in a curiously significant way to some of the already established connections between the play and the Harvey-Nashe literature. For Eliot and Florio were somehow involved in the Harvey-Nashe controversy, and in Gabriel Harvey's *Pierces Supererogation*—which is the very pamphlet from which Shakespeare quotes a joke in *Love's Labour's Lost*—a long speech is made by a person who is anonymous but who has been identified quite unmistakably as John Eliot. This Eliot speech in *Pierces Supererogation* is concerned with a discussion of Nashe's style which is described as the style of a "villanist", of one experienced in the ways of the world, and is favourably contrasted with the "artist" styles of writing preferred by learned persons. "Art" and "artist" are here used in the Elizabethan sense of "learning" and "learned". If these remarks of Eliot's, as quoted by Harvey, are compared with the speeches in which Berowne deplores excessive book-learning, it is noticed that—although there is all the difference in the world between Shakespeare's poetry and the jargon in which Harvey reports Eliot's views—the arguments in both cases are very similar. The possibility thus begins to dawn that as Shakespeare appears to have agreed with Eliot in not liking Florio and the Protestant refugee language-teachers, so he might have agreed with

him in not caring for the "artist" style of Harvey. Harvey
has been suspected as one of the "originals" of Holofernes
or Armado, and the probability that he and Nashe are often
alluded to in the play increases, rather than diminishes, the
probability that Eliot's joke against Florio and the foreign
pedagogues is also alluded to in it, since there were connections of some kind between Eliot and Harvey and
between Florio and Nashe.

The Eliot speech in *Pierces Supererogation* bridges yet
another gap. For I believe that there are unmistakable
connections between it and George Chapman's dedication
to his *Shadow of Night*. Chapman there argues in the
opposite direction—exalting, in effect, the "artist" against
the "villanist", though he does not actually use those
terms—and certain verbal coincidences convince me that
he is in fact answering Eliot's speech. If so, he must have
thought that he, as well as Florio and Harvey, was one
of the "artists" of whose style Eliot did not approve. We
thus have Florio, Harvey, Chapman, the three most likely
"originals" for the satire on pedantry in Holofernes and
Armado, grouped together for us by Eliot, and I suggest
that the Pedant and Braggart masks do contain hits at all
three.

I need not again remind the reader that an attack on
Raleigh's "School of Night", of which Chapman's *Shadow
of Night* was an expression, is now thought by most authori-
ties to be at the core of the topical meaning of *Love's
Labour's Lost*. And our chain of reasoning—passing from
Florio to Eliot, from Eliot to Harvey, from Harvey to
Chapman—has led us straight to this core. This confirms the
belief that the Eliot-Florio clues to the play are valid clues.

We now return to Florio and remind ourselves of another
fact about him, namely his friendship with Bruno.

Bruno was a somewhat daring innovator in the realm
of thought and an early believer in the Copernican system.
There are indications that at least one member of the

"School of Night"—Thomas Hariot—knew of Bruno's work and it is my belief that the Italian philosopher exercised a considerable influence on Raleigh and his associates. Through his association with Bruno, therefore, Florio would have some right to be satirised as a Copernican and a mathematical and philosophical fantastic, along with Hariot, Raleigh, Chapman, and the other members of the "school" upon which the play touches. Moreover, Florio had recalled in one of his manuals some memories of rude things which Bruno had said about England and English universities in his book called the *Cena de le ceneri* which was a plea for the Copernican system. Therefore, there is a memory of Bruno's Copernican dialogues in the Eliot-Florio controversy; and this gives us a connection between the stars and the schoolmasters in the play.

The study of Bruno and Florio can also do much to elucidate the connection between the stars and the ladies' eyes in the play. When in England, Bruno addressed to Sidney an anti-Petrarchistic tirade against writing sonnets to women, although he knew of Sir Philip's passion for "Stella" and of the sonnets which he was addressing to her. This is alluded to by Florio in the last dialogue of his *Second Fruits* in which he sets out arguments for and against love, the Petrarchist and anti-Petrarchist dispute which was a commonplace of the Italian Renaissance. I am convinced that this dialogue was carefully studied by Shakespeare and that there are undoubted echoes of it in the arguments for and against love and sonnet-writing in *Love's Labour's Lost*. Shakespeare not only knew of this dialogue, he knew of the history behind it and that it referred to Bruno's attacks on sonnet-writing and to Sidney's "Stella". In the play, Shakespeare is defending "Stella" from the indirect attacks of Bruno, the Copernican, and that is one of the explanations of the "stars-eyes" antithesis which is so constantly recurring. With this there fit in certain echoes of *Astrophel and Stella* which are to be detected in the play.

And such a gallant defence of "Stella" from the aspersions of astronomers and "artists" would come very naturally from a member of the Essex-Southampton group engaged in satirising the Raleigh group. For "Stella" was the Lady Penelope Rich, *née* Devereux, the sister of the Earl of Essex.

This thesis is remarkably confirmed and further amplified by an important and hitherto unpublished document which I have come across in the Record Office. This is an essay by the Earl of Northumberland, a noted member of the "School of Night" and one of those mentioned by Chapman in the dedication to the *Shadow of Night*, on the subject of love and learning. It appears to be addressed to his wife, who was the sister of "Stella" and of the Earl of Essex, and he tells her that he has abandoned love and the writing of "platts" for ladies, imitated from Sidney, for study, particularly the scientific study of light. I am certain that it will be admitted that it is the argument of this essay which Shakespeare is reversing and contradicting in *Love's Labour's Lost*. Both the Devereux sisters had thus been insulted by "artists" and Shakespeare is defending both of them by his allusions to "stars" and "light".

I think, further, that the immediate inspiration of both *Love's Labour's Lost* and of the Earl of Northumberland's essay were the Gray's Inn Revels of 1594–5 with their mock speeches in praise, alternately, of study and of pleasure. Northumberland, Essex, Southampton, Rich, and their ladies attended these revels and so did Shakespeare, since one of his plays was acted during the course of them. Both Eliot's *Ortho-epia Gallica* and the well-known *Willobie His Avisa* are probably linked in some way with *Gesta Grayorum*. Many of the minor jokes in the play are, I believe, Gray's Inn gossip and slang, and it was written some time during 1595, after the revels.

Such is the rough outline of the argument. It uses all the best-accredited of the theories hitherto extant concerning the topical satire in the play—the Florio theory, the Harvey-Nashe theory, the "School of Night" theory, the Gray's Inn Revels theory—and it supplements them by certain missing links, the most important of which are Eliot and his *Ortho-epia Gallica*, the Earl of Northumberland and his essay, and a clearer understanding of Bruno and of his reputation in England.

The conclusion to which it leads us is that, although there are no definite "portraits" of individuals in *Love's Labour's Lost*, it is full of allusions to contemporaries. The play is written against the "School of Night", but with the emphasis on Northumberland, rather than on Raleigh. In the four male characters are reflections of Raleigh and his friends and of Southampton and his friends, and also some vague memory of Bruno. The eyes of the ladies frequently recall the eyes of "Stella" and of her sister. The comic characters mirror, without losing their identities, the dependent "artists" of the "School of Night", Chapman, Hariot, and perhaps others, also Harvey and Nashe, and Eliot's joke against Florio and the foreign schoolmasters. Florio is most important in the play in all kinds of connections.

The deductions as to Shakespeare's life which can be made from this argument, if it is accepted, are that he undoubtedly was an adherent of the Essex-Southampton group and opposed to Raleigh, Northumberland and their friends, that Chapman is indeed the "rival poet" of the sonnets, and that Eliot and Florio were important influences in the earlier part of his career. I suggest that Eliot may have been one of the Catholic teachers or dependents surrounding the Earl of Southampton who were suppressed and supplanted by Protestants, such as Florio, put in by Burleigh, and, if so, it would look as though Shakespeare's sympathy was with the Catholics in that household—a sympathy which he is possibly expressing in *Love's Labour's Lost*, though in very guarded and indirect ways as befitted the extreme danger of such an attitude.

CHAPTER I

Florio

The most frequently repeated objection to the possibility of the presence of satire on Florio in *Love's Labour's Lost* has always been that the Earl of Southampton was both Florio's and Shakespeare's patron. The first edition of the Italian scholar's dictionary, the *Worlde of Wordes*, was dedicated to Southampton in 1598 and from the preface it appears that Florio had been in the earl's "paie and patronage" as his tutor in modern languages, particularly Italian, for some years. Is it likely, asked Malone and many others after him, that Shakespeare would have held up to ridicule this man who was his patron's tutor and protégé?

Now this objection, reasonable though it sounds, can be demolished because it rests upon a misconception. It assumes that Southampton himself chose Florio to be his tutor and friend, an assumption which a more careful examination of the circumstances attendant upon Florio's entry into the Southampton household will soon show to be entirely unwarranted.

Southampton's father had died when his son and heir was only eight years old. The young third earl was thus a minor during the earlier part of his tenure of the title and did not come of age until 1594. Minors in noble families automatically became royal wards, and William Cecil, Lord Burleigh, as Master of the Queen's Wards, appointed himself Southampton's guardian.[1] As guardian,

[1] See A. K. Gray, "The Secret of *Love's Labour's Lost*", in *Publications of the Modern Language Association of America*, XXXIX, p. 582.

Burleigh would have the right to choose Southampton's tutors and to supervise his education. Florio was certainly in Southampton's household by 1594[1] and there is thus good reason to suppose that his appointment to the post was made by Burleigh during Southampton's minority. This is rendered more probable by the fact that Florio's antecedents suggest him as a person whom Burleigh would have been very likely to choose for such a position. His father had at one time lived in Burleigh's house and he himself is suspected of having worked for Burleigh and Walsingham under cover of his employment at the French embassy as tutor to the ambassador's daughter.

Southampton came of a Catholic family. He was probably christened according to Catholic rites and his father's Catholic friends would have surrounded him in early youth. Among these friends was a family called Wells, sons of Thomas Wells of Bambridge, near Winchester. Gilbert Wells was one of the executors to Southampton's father's will.[2] Now when Burleigh, champion and mainstay of Protestantism and of the Elizabethan settlement, became guardian to the young earl he would naturally try to draw him away from these influences. According to the late Mrs Stopes "Lord Burleigh could inculcate conformity to the Queen's will in matters of religion without undue harshness; and we may be sure that never more would the boy have the courage to refuse to be present at the reading of the English service".[3] It does not take much imagination to see here the elements of a schism within Southampton's household, his father's friends aligned against the creatures put in by a guardian too powerful to resist openly. The suspicion with which Burleigh regarded the

[1] *John Florio*, p. 125.
[2] C. C. Stopes, *Henry, Third Earl of Southampton*, 1922, pp. 5, 15. The other executors were Charles Paget, Edward Gage, Ralph Hare and Thomas Dymocke.
[3] *Op. cit.* p. 18.

Wells family is more than once hinted at in the Salisbury Papers. Amongst recusants in the county of Southampton in 1592 were

> Gilbert Wells of Twiford, esquire.
> Henry Wells of Bewlie....[1]

And one of the Cecil spies, writing to Burleigh in August, 1587, said:

> There dwelleth in Purbeck a brother of Gilbert Wells, the recusant, by whom, or near to his house, it is thought there is a passage to and fro of very bad men.[2]

There can be no doubt that the Earl of Southampton's guardian kept a careful watch upon his ward's Catholic friends.

The fight between the new guardian and the old friends of the family would reach its climax over the most vital question of all, the education of the young earl. In which faith was he to be brought up? The Countess de Chambrun was the first to point out the significance in this connection of Swithin Wells.[3]

Swithin Wells was a brother of Gilbert Wells. Like the rest of his family he was a Catholic[4] and at one time he kept a school at Monkton Farleigh, near Bath, for the sons of gentlemen.[5] Early in 1582, the Privy Council ordered

---

[1] *Hist. MSS. Commission, Salisbury Papers*, IV, pp. 270–1.

[2] *Ibid.* III, p. 279. Francis Kellwey to Lord Burleigh.

[3] In her letter to the *Times Literary Supplement* of 11 October 1934, p. 695.

[4] He said at his examination in 1586 that he had only been a Catholic for three years. This cannot have been true, for he was described in 1582 as a dangerous Papist and is known to have come of a Catholic family. His object in making this untrue statement at his examination was probably to shield his pupils.

[5] S.P.12. 192. No. 18. This document and other State Papers concerning Swithin Wells are printed in full in *Unpublished Documents relating to the English Martyrs*, ed. J. H. Pollen, I, pp. 131–3. Catholic Record Society, 1908.

the sheriff of Wiltshire to search for "one Welles, a
schoolemaster and a daungerous Papiste".[1] It appears that
his school was a Catholic school, as indeed the Catholic
source relates with pride:

> After his marriage, Mr Wells for some years employed himself
> in teaching belles-lettres and music, having for his servant and
> assistant therein Mr Woodfen, afterwards priest and martyr, and
> he had the comfort of training up many of them in the true faith;
> and amongst others, several who were afterwards priests, and
> religious, and some martyrs, till at length he was obliged by the
> malice of his enemies and of the ministers to quit this employ-
> ment.[2]

The same authority, just before this passage describing the
school, tells us something about Swithin Wells's activities
before he started the school at Monkton Farleigh. In his
youth he was educated at home in the "liberal sciences" and
then went to Italy, partly as a pilgrimage and partly "to
learn the language". On his return to England,

> he was employed in the service of several persons of quality, and
> after some time, for his skill in languages and for his eloquence,
> was desired by the most noble Earl of Southampton, a most con-
> stant professor of the Catholic faith, to live in his house, as he did,
> much to his own commendation for several years.[3]

Now since this happened *before* Wells had the school at
Monkton Farleigh, which he started about 1576,[4] the Earl
of Southampton here referred to must be the second earl
and not, as the Countess de Chambrun thought, the third
earl who was Florio's pupil and Shakespeare's patron. The
description "a constant professor of the Catholic faith"

[1] *Acts of the Privy Council*, New Series, XIII, p. 403.
[2] R. Challoner, *Martyrs to the Catholic Faith, Memoirs of Missionary
Priests*, 1878 edition, I, 277.
[3] *Op. cit., loc. cit.*
[4] He stated at his examination in 1586 (S.P.12. 192. No. 18) that
he had kept the school "for the space of vj yeares or thereabowts"
and we know that it was stopped in 1582.

fits the second earl better than it does his son who, although brought up as a Catholic, eventually lapsed. But the second earl very probably invited Swithin Wells into his house for the benefit of his young family and he may well have been the tutor whom he hoped would help to guide his son's education after his death. Swithin Wells was certainly living in Southampton House about 1587, long after the third earl had come into the title, for in a list of recusants and suspected persons in the Domestic State Papers, undated but assigned with good reason to 1587 by the Calendar, we read

> Swythen Welles lodging in Southampton howse.[1]

Moreover, Swithin himself stated on 9 August 1586 that, since giving up his school at Monkton Farleigh, he had

> lyved amongest his frends, and now lyveth upon the benevolence of his frends, as of his brother Gilbert Wells & others of his frends.[2]

As we have seen, Gilbert Wells had been a friend of Southampton's father and was one of the executors to the will, so the young earl himself was probably the real bene-factor whom Swithin hesitated to name here. As Swithin Wells had been a schoolmaster, had a good knowledge of Italian, and was evidently a highly cultured person, it seems probable that the relations between him and the young Southampton were, for a time, those of tutor and pupil. He would have been a likely choice of the Catholic party in the Southampton ménage for such a position.

But such a choice would obviously not suit Burleigh, the Protestant guardian. Swithin Wells was a suspected person. He was closely questioned in August 1586 as to

[1] S.P.12. 206. No. 74. See *Cal. S.P. Dom.*, 1581–1590, p. 448.
[2] *Unpublished Documents relating to the English Martyrs*, ed. J. H. Pollen, I, 132.

his knowledge of Babington and Savage. Savage he said he did not know at all, but he admitted to an acquaintance with Babington, though not otherwise than "in saluting one an other by name as the(y) mett in the stretes".[1] He was a frequenter of Mrs Bellamy's house at Harrow,[2] where Babington was captured. But there was, apparently, not enough evidence against him for a conviction in 1587. Three years later they caught him. By then Wells had taken a house in Holborn near Gray's Inn Fields at which priests were received. There, one day, Topcliffe and his myrmidons rushing in found mass in the act of being celebrated. All those present were arrested and sent to gaol. Swithin Wells was out at the time of the domiciliary visit but on his return he went to Justice Young to complain of the treatment of his friends and was himself arrested. A batch of executions followed in due course. Plasden, White and some others met their ends at Tyburn, but Swithin Wells and Edmund Gennings, *alias* Ironmonger, were dispatched in the usual gruesome manner on 10 December 1591, in Gray's Inn Fields outside Wells's house.[3]

At some date which is uncertain, but it was some time before 1594, John Florio became tutor in modern languages, particularly Italian, to the Earl of Southampton. There are various reasons which I have detailed elsewhere[4]

[1] *Unpublished Documents relating to the English Martyrs, loc. cit.*

[2] *Ibid., loc. cit.*

[3] R. Challoner gives a full and most interesting account of Swithin Wells (*op. cit.* I, 180–7, 276–8) which is based on manuscript sources. But as I notice that Mr Conyers Read labels Challoner "uncritical" (*Bibliography of British History, Tudor Period,* 1485–1603, 1933, No. 1629), I have only dwelt on points in his story—the school and the connection with Southampton—which are corroborated by the *Acts of the Privy Council* and by the Domestic State Papers. The manner of Wells's end is attested by (besides Challoner) such varied and unimpeachable authorities as *Calendar of Domestic State Papers,* 1591–1594, pp. 151–2; *Douai Diaries,* ed. T. F. Knox, 1878, I, p. 243; John Stow, *Annales, or Generall Chronicle of England,* 1615, p. 764.   [4] *John Florio,* pp. 83–6, 216–18.

and which need not now be repeated for thinking that Florio was probably an agent of the Cecils. He had recently been employed at the French embassy and had almost certainly used his position there to obtain information for Walsingham. What part he may have played in such an episode as the discovery of the Babington plot one can only conjecture, but he seems to have boasted in his old age to his friend William Vaughan of his prowess in the destruction of Jesuits and Papists. Undoubtedly he was a very "safe" Protestant. Burleigh as guardian had the right, as has already been said, to appoint tutors and to supervise the education of his ward. There can be very little doubt that Florio was put into Southampton's household by Burleigh.

What did the earl himself think about it all? "Without undue harshness", said Mrs Stopes, "Burleigh could inculcate conformity to the Queen's will." But it cannot have been altogether pleasant to have to stand by and say nothing while his Catholic language tutor was hanged and disembowelled not far from the Southampton town house, to be succeeded[1] by a Protestant tutor who was probably also a spy and whose appointment he was quite powerless to resist. The Earl of Southampton's religious convictions were not perhaps very deeply rooted; he seems eventually, much later than this, to have become a Protestant. But he was not too fond of his guardian—nothing would induce him to marry Burleigh's grand-daughter—and he was never a very contented subject of Queen Elizabeth. It is well within the bounds of possibility that Florio's presence in his house was almost unbearably irksome to him.

It has been necessary to tell this story in some detail in order to demonstrate that a caricature of Florio by Shakespeare need not necessarily have been displeasing to South-

---

[1] Burleigh, of course, need not have waited until the death of Wells before appointing Florio.

ampton, and that the old objection to Warburton's theory on the grounds that the earl was both Florio's and Shakespeare's patron is quite misleading.

*   *   *   *

Our next task must be to collect and present to the reader the various arguments which have been urged in the past by those who have believed that Shakespeare was laughing at Florio in *Love's Labour's Lost*.

The most prominent of these rests upon the occurrence in the play of the "Venetia" proverb. "Facile precor gelida quando pecus omne sub umbra Ruminat" misquotes[1] Holofernes to display his acquaintance with Mantuan, and he follows this up immediately with a proverb in Italian:

> Ah, good old Mantuan! I may speak of thee as the traveller doth of Venice:
>
> Venetia, Venetia,
> Chi non ti vede, non ti pretia.
> Old Mantuan! old Mantuan! Who understandeth thee not, loves thee not.[2]

Many people have pointed out that this proverb is to be found in Florio's conversation manual designed to teach Italian to Englishmen which he called the *Second Fruits* (1591). The Countess de Chambrun noted that he also gives it in his earlier manual, the *First Fruits* (1578). In the *First Fruits* the "Venetia" saying occurs as one of a number of proverbs which Florio borrowed from James Sanford's *Garden of Pleasure*; in the *Second Fruits* it is grouped with some other aphorisms on "travel".

Attention has also been drawn to the following phrase in the *First Fruits*:

> We neede not speak so much of loue, al books are ful of loue, with so many authours, that it were labour lost to speake of Loue.[3]

---

[1] See Professor Dover Wilson's note, the Cambridge *New Shakespeare*, *L.L.L.* pp. 155–6.

[2] IV. ii. 99–105.   [3] *First Fruits*, sig. S 3.

It is suggested that this is where Shakespeare found his
title of *Love's Labour's Lost*.

Holofernes is addicted to uttering strings of synonyms
and on one occasion in particular he talks exactly "like a
dictionary".

> ...like a jewel in the ear of caelo, the sky, the welkin, the
> heaven, and anon falleth like a crab on the face of terra, the soil,
> the land, the earth.[1]

Those who have thought that this might be an allusion
to Florio's Italian-English dictionary have had it objected
to them that his *Worlde of Wordes* was not published until
1598 which is at least one year later than the latest date
at which *Love's Labour's Lost* can possibly have been composed. But Florio had announced in 1591 that his dictionary was nearly ready and he says himself in the preface
to the 1598 edition that people have been ridiculing this
"child of his invention" (the dictionary) before its birth,
or publication.

> ...I more then feare much detracting: for I haue already
> tasted some, and that extraordinarie though in an ordinarie place,
> where my childe was beaten ere it was borne: some diuining of
> his imperfectnes for his English part; some fore-speaking his
> generall weakenes, and very gently seeming to pitie his fathers.
> And one auerring he could beget a better of his owne.[2]

Florio's dictionary seems to have been a subject of gossip
in taverns or "ordinaries" before publication and Holofernes's parody of the dictionary manner cannot therefore
be disposed of as an allusion to Florio on chronological
grounds.

To these well-worn arguments the Countess de Chambrun has more recently added the ingenious observation

---

[1] IV. ii. 4–7.
[2] *John Florio*, pp. 212, 340.

that it is possible to construe "Holofernes" into a kind of anagram of Florio's name:

IHOLOFERNES = IOHNESFLOREO.[1]

This is certainly curious, but the deciphering, or fancied deciphering, of Elizabethan anagrams has led to so many extraordinary theories that cautious-minded persons are wisely reluctant to build much upon evidence of this kind.

The rest of the case for Florio as an "original" of Holofernes or of Armado has rested mainly on questions of style. Florio was a great believer in proverbs; he loved synonyms and never used one word if there was any chance of using two or three; he was something of a euphuist—in a word, he was pedantic, precious and affected as any reader of his dedications can see for themselves. *Love's Labour's Lost* is a satire on pedantry, preciosity, and affectation and this, taken in conjunction with the "Venetia" proverb, the title, and, possibly, the anagram is enough to show—so it has been said—that satire on Florio is present in the play.

From our new general knowledge of Florio's life and opinions some points might be added to this argument. It has been suggested, for instance, that because Holofernes takes the rôle of Judas Maccabaeus in the masque of the Worthies and in the course of acting that part is made to say "Judas I am"[2] three times amid the jeers and interruptions of the audience, therefore the "original" of Holofernes might have been a "false friend"[3] or a "known informer".[4] Holofernes also intercepts and reads a letter, with the approval of Sir Nathaniel, the parson, who says: "Sir, you have done this in the fear of God, very religiously."[5] Those who have made these suggestions have

---

[1] *Giovanni Florio*, p. 167; *Shakespeare Actor-Poet*, p. 128. A somewhat similar suggestion was put forward by C. J. Fèret in *Fulham Old and New*, 1900, I, 119. [2] v. ii. 591–604.
[3] H. D. Gray, *The Original Version of "Love's Labour's Lost"*, Leland Stanford Junior Publications, 1918, p. 18.
[4] Rupert Taylor, *The Date of "Love's Labour's Lost"*, 1932, p. 122.
[5] IV. ii. 153–4.

not known that Florio, the original "original", might possibly lay claim to hits of this kind. We have suspected Florio of having played the part of a spy during his employment at the French embassy and if something of this had leaked out it would have made him somewhat eligible for the reproach of "Judas I am", particularly if he was also really working for Burleigh in the Southampton household.

Holofernes, again, is a most supercilious critic in all matters appertaining to literary taste, and so also was Florio. He judged the drama from the "classical" point of view, deploring the mingling of tragedy and comedy, the lack of "decorum", the disregard for the unities, which he observed on the English stage.

Henry.	The plaies that they plaie in England, are not right comedies.
Thomas.	Yet they doo nothing else but plaie euery daye.
Henry.	Yea but they are neither right comedies, nor right tragedies.
Giovanni.	How would you name them then?
Henry.	Representations of histories without any decorum.[1]

Farmer thought that these remarks were aimed at Shakespeare and that it was Florio who had thereby "given the first affront" to the dramatist.[2] To this it used to be objected that Shakespeare had written no plays as early as 1591 when this criticism of the English stage was published. This is not quite so cogent as it once was, since modern scholarship is tending to date the beginning of Shakespeare's career as a dramatist rather earlier than used to be thought possible. Mr Peter Alexander, for instance, thinks that the commencement of his first period should be dated "some considerable time before 1589".[3] But whether or not Florio was thinking of Shakespeare in the *Second Fruits* in 1591, the remarks which he made then are

---

[1] *Second Fruits*, sig. D4.   [2] Furness, *op. cit.* p. 352.
[3] Peter Alexander, *Shakespeare's Henry VI and Richard III*, Shakespeare Problems Series, 1929, p. 200.

typical of his constant attitude to the drama. He remained
an adherent of the "classical", a supporter of Jonson's
"art" rather than of Shakespeare's "nature", throughout
his life. His pose of cultured contempt for the crude
barbarism, the disregard of all those rules which governed
the drama in less backward countries, which held sway in
England may have been at times somewhat trying to those
who were "natural" and not "artistic" dramatists.

The argument of the similarity of Holofernes's and
Armado's style to that of Florio might be elaborated at
some length, for there is reason to think that not only did
Florio use proverbs, synonyms, and every kind of Italianate,
Spanish, euphuistic and arcadian device in his own writings,
but that he deliberately taught such ornaments to his
pupils, and therefore would be a peculiarly suitable object
for satire on literary affectations. I have collected a number
of passages which suggest to me that some of Armado's
fantasies recall Florio's translations from Guevara in the
First Fruits. Various linguistic or grammatical points
touched upon in the play could also be construed as allusions
to Florio's teaching manuals. The Countess de Chambrun
has mentioned Costard's "honorificabilitudinitatibus" in
connection with some remarks of Florio's on the use of
long words in Italian. She also compares Florio's views
on apostrophes with Holofernes's on "the apostrophus".[1]
One might add to this that Florio complains of the difficulty of learning to pronounce English owing to the fact
that all the letters in the words are not sounded, as they
are in Italian.[2] It will be remembered that Holofernes
grumbles at those who will pronounce "dout" instead of
"doubt", "det" instead of "debt" and so on.[3]

---

[1] *Giovanni Florio*, pp. 166–7; *Shakespeare Actor-Poet*, pp. 127–8.

[2] "...qvanto al proferirla [la lingua inglese], ella é contrarja à la
nostra, perche se una parola é di molte lettere non si proferiscono,
tutte la qval cosa è causa che ella é dificile à imparare." *First Fruits*,
sigs. Ss4 and Ss4v. [3] v. i. 19–24.

But one can go on in this way indefinitely, citing small points and small parallels, without ever really succeeding in *proving* that the satire in *Love's Labour's Lost* is aimed particularly at Florio rather than at some other affected person of Shakespeare's acquaintance or at affectation in general. In fact the whole case for the presence of Florio in the play is still unconvincing. If Shakespeare called his pedant "Holofernes" after the pedant in Rabelais he might well have done so without noticing the Countess de Chambrun's anagram. The stock pedant of Italian popular comedy used dictionary terms, proverbs, long words, and scraps of quotation. Other people have argued, and not unconvincingly, that the affectations of Holofernes and Armado were meant to recall those of Harvey or of Chapman. Almost all Elizabethans indulged in stylistic extravagances of one kind or another. In short, although the initial barrier to the possibility of Florio's presence in the play has been removed, his case remains highly inconclusive. I think one would be justified in saying that Shakespeare's quotation of the "Venetia" proverb suggests that he may have had modern-language manuals, such as Florio's, in view, as well as Latin colloquies and eclogues, when poking fun at school textbooks in general. But farther than that it is not as yet safe to venture.

*   *   *   *

At this point we begin to bring forward some entirely fresh evidence and the first new witness in this case who is waiting to be called is Florio's friend William Vaughan.

Vaughan introduced Florio by name into his fantasia called *The Golden Fleece*, published in 1626. He describes Florio as having been called to appear before Apollo to defend himself from a charge which has been brought against him, namely that in a certain "litany" which he had recited he had descended to a frivolity of tone and matter unsuited to a person of his gravity. Florio defends himself by arguing that it is sometimes necessary to temper gravity with brightness to suit the tastes of one's pupils and patrons. Apollo gave judgment in Florio's favour and in so doing referred to him as an "ingenuous Scholler".[1]

Now there is an earlier work by Vaughan called *The Spirit of Detraction* (1611) in which there is no mention at all of Florio by name but in which complaint is made of the manner in which an "ingenuous scholler"—exactly the expression used to describe Florio in the other book—has been satirised on the stage:

> Herein our common *Stage-players* and *Comicke-writers* haue as many witnesses as the world hath eyes, that all kind of persons, without respect of sexe or degree are nickt and nipped, rayled and reuiled by these snarling curre-dogs. For let a man endeuour to walke vprightly in the sight of *God*, separating himselfe as neere as he can from tatling tospots and Tobacconists, loth to sit in the seat of the scornefull and vnrighteous, lest he become like will to like, and especially loth to communicate in the *Eucharist* with such notorious and prophane persons; presently these Ganders gagle, that such a one is an hypocrite, or a peeuish puritane. Let a man be silent, putting the barre of discretion before his lips, lest his tongue trippe, and procure hurt, according to that:
>
> > —*Nulli tacuisse nocet, nocet esse locutum.*
>
> No hurt by silence comes: but speech brings hurt:
>
> These muttering *Momes* paint (*sic*) out, that he is a meacocke, a melancholicke Mummer, or a simple sot. Let an ingenuous scholler salted with experience, seasoned with Christian doctrine, hauing his heart seared and sealed with zeale and charity, let him but broach forth the barrell of his wit, which *God* hath giuen him; they crie out that his braine is but an empty barrell, his wit but barren, his matter borrowed out of other mens bookes.[2]

---

[1] *John Florio*, p. 263.
[2] W. Vaughan, *The Spirit of Detraction*, 1611, sig. P3v.

Now the melancholy person who is not a "Tobacconist" herein described may perhaps be Vaughan himself.[1] But what of the "ingenuous scholler" whom the comedians have laughed at for broaching "the barrell of his wit"? When Vaughan introduced his friend Florio *by name* into his later book *The Golden Fleece* he described him in one place as an "ingenuous Scholler",[2] the very words used here. I therefore suggest that in the passage just quoted Vaughan may be alluding to some presentation of Florio on the stage. The conceit of "broaching the barrell" of one's wit was congenial to Florio, judging by his ludicrous elaboration of the proverb "La botte dà di quello che hà" in his letter to Windebank.[3] And, what is still more significant, it is a conceit which gave great delight to Holofernes.

Jaquenetta.	God give you good morrow, Master Person.
Holofernes.	Master Person—quasi pierce-one? And if one should be pierced, which is the one?
Costard.	Marry, master schoolmaster, he that is likeliest to a hogshead.
Holofernes.	Piercing a hogshead! a good lustre of conceit in a turf of earth, fire enough for a flint, pearl enough for a swine: 'tis pretty, it is well.[4]

[1] Vaughan was a melancholic who disapproved of tobacco. But Florio was a smoker (see *John Florio*, pp. 251, 332) and, although a grave personage, was willing to adapt himself to the lighter humours of his clients, as occasion demanded. (*Ibid.* p. 262.)

[2] Florio has been defending before Apollo his "litany", which some have called frivolous, and Apollo pronounces judgment in his favour in these words:

"*Apollo*, after that *Florio* had thus defended his cause, yeelded his censure in these few words: Whosoeuer goes about to depriue men of all kinde of pleasure, seekes to depriue them of freedome and of a cheerefull nature, which God preferres before a sullen crabbed mind, as was that of *Caius*. Beeing tempred, it consorts well in an ingenuous Scholler...." (*The Golden Fleece*, sig. Dd 2 v.)

[3] *John Florio*, pp. 293–4.

[4] IV. ii. 85–93.

Vaughan's evidence, although far from clear and certain, seems to me on the whole to point rather towards a confirmation of the presence of Florio in *Love's Labour's Lost*.

*   *   *   *

The next new witness has some much more important information to impart.

John Eliot's *Ortho-epia Gallica*, published in 1593,[1] appears on the surface to be a language manual for teaching French to Englishmen. Like so many other Elizabethan language manuals, including those of Florio, it consists largely of sets of dialogues on various subjects which are printed both in English and in the language which the book is concerned to teach, in this case French. But on closer examination this *Ortho-epia Gallica* which poses so innocently as a harmless modern-language textbook turns out to be quite other than it seems. In reality it is an attack on the many foreign teachers of languages then in London. These foreigners were, for the most part, Protestant refugees who had come to live in England to escape the inquisition in their own countries. Many of them made a living by teaching their languages in London and they published numerous manuals and grammars for the use of their pupils. These are the people against whom Eliot's *Ortho-epia Gallica* is directed. Their methods and pretensions are openly criticised in some of his earlier dialogues and their manuals are cleverly parodied throughout his book. Chief among Eliot's victims is the celebrated Italian teacher John Florio who, like the majority of the foreigners then in London, was of Protestant refugee origin, and merciless fun is poked at his two books of Italian-English dialogues, the *First Fruits* and the *Second Fruits*.

Now this fact, that in 1593 there was published an attack on Florio and a parody of his two manuals, is

---

[1] This paragraph is a summary of *John Florio*, chapter VII, where the evidence for these statements is set out.

something which has been quite unknown to all those who have hitherto theorised concerning the presence of the Italian in *Love's Labour's Lost*. But once this is known the whole complexion of the case is immediately altered. Florio no longer appears as an aloof teacher and scholar who would not be likely to excite ridicule. He becomes at once *topical*. Any time after April 1593 an allusion to Eliot's parody of him would be an amusing topical hit of the very kind which Shakespeare is constantly making in this intensely topical comedy. And if any points of contact between Eliot's and Shakespeare's satire of Florio could be detected, the case for the presence of the Italian in *Love's Labour's Lost* would be enormously strengthened. Let us therefore now hasten to compare the jokes of Eliot with those of Shakespeare.

It will be remembered that Florio's phrase "it were labour lost to speake of Loue" has been suggested as the origin of the title *Love's Labour's Lost*. The full title of Eliot's manual is "*Ortho-epia Gallica*, ELIOTS FRVITS *for the French*" which is obviously, when the true nature of the book is understood, a reminder of the titles of Florio's *First Fruits* and *Second Fruits*. Both Eliot and Shakespeare thus seem to recall Florio in their titles.

Next, the quotation of the "Venetia" proverb by Holofernes takes on a new significance when it is known that the two works in which Florio used it had recently been parodied by Eliot. The mention of "the traveller" in connection with this proverb is also, I think, significant.

> Ah, good old Mantuan! I may speak of thee as *the traveller*
>   doth of Venice:
> Venetia, Venetia,
> Chi non ti vede, non ti pretia.

Eliot's longest and closest parody of Florio is in his second dialogue which he calls "The Traueller".[1] Shakespeare's

---

[1] *John Florio*, pp. 155–64.

mention of "the traveller" in the same breath as Florio's proverb therefore, in my opinion, underscores the whole allusion and brings it into line with Eliot's burlesque.[1]

We have seen that Hunter suggested that the expression "With that face", used of Armado, might be an allusion to Florio's countenance of which Cornwallis gave an unflattering description. The face of Holofernes also receives harsh treatment in the play.

Holofernes.	I will not be put out of countenance.
Berowne.	Because thou hast no face.
Holofernes.	What is this?
Boyet.	A cittern-head.[2]
Dumaine.	The head of a bodkin.
Berowne.	A death's face in a ring.
Longaville.	The face of an old Roman coin, scarce seen.
Boyet.	The pummel of Cæsar's falchion.
Dumaine.	The carved-bone face on a flask.
Berowne.	St. George's half-cheek in a brooch.[3]

Now one of Eliot's dialogues is called "The Painter"; in it the speakers describe the portraits on view in the painter's shop and I have suggested elsewhere[4] that one of these descriptions may be a caricature of Florio's appearance.

It is an Italian Harlekin.
He is beleeue me, verie vvell counterfeited for a foole.
He is not verie vvell shadowed for a wise man.
What vvanteth there?
He is crump-shouldered and crooked, and hath a Hawkes-nose.

---

[1] It is perhaps also significant that when Jonson alluded to the *Second Fruits* in his *Volpone* he too should have insisted on its rules for travel. See *John Florio*, pp. 132–3, 279.

[2] In connection with this, attention has been drawn to the phrase "Car elle avoit visage de rebec" in Rabelais, Book II, chapter III. See Huntington Brown, *Rabelais in English Literature*, 1933, p. 210.

[3] v. ii. 605–14.

[4] *John Florio*, pp. 167–8, 210.

The Persians adored those who had an Aquiline nose, for Cyrus sake, who they say, had his of forme like a shooing-horne.

He hath his hands very crooked and limy fingerd.

For all that he is not a theefe.

What can he do?

He can hold his peace and keepe his owne counsell.[1]

Both on account of its resemblance to Cornwallis's description of Florio ("he looks more like a good fellow than a wise man") and also because Florio retorts to his enemies in his dictionary preface to *"goe to the Painters shop, or looking-glasse of* Ammianus Marcellinus" if they want a description of themselves, it is very probable that Eliot was maliciously hinting at Florio here. Eliot's words suggest features aquiline in outline, and hard and bony in texture; this is more or less borne out by the extant portrait of Florio, and it also fairly well fits the unflattering description of Holofernes given by his tormentors. But perhaps most significant of all is the remark made by Dumaine as he watches Armado as Hector.

He's a god or a painter; for he makes faces.[2]

This was a proverb, but might it not also have recalled Eliot's painter's shop?

Eliot was a great admirer and imitator of Rabelais whom he mentions by name and from whom he frequently quotes.[3] Indeed, his whole joke against Florio and the foreign teachers is conceived in a Rabelaisian style. For example,

---

[1] *Ortho-epia Gallica,* sigs. *k2, k3; Parlement of Pratlers,* pp. 63–4. (Note. *The Parlement of Pratlers* is the title of a reprint of some extracts from *Ortho-epia Gallica,* edited by Jack Lindsay and published by the Fanfrolico Press in 1928. Whenever the passage quoted in the text occurs in this reprint, page references to it are given, as well as signature references to the original.)

[2] v. ii. 642–3.

[3] Eliot's debt to Rabelais has recently been studied in detail by Huntington Brown, *Rabelais in English Literature,* 1933, pp. 43–7, 216–20.

the serious manuals nearly always contained a dialogue about a meal in which was taught the vocabulary relating to food and drink. Eliot recalls and parodies these serious meal scenes in a dialogue which he entitles "The Drunken Mens Banket", and which he fills with quotations from Rabelais exalting wine as the fountain of wit and poetry.

Tarry a little that I deduce a dram out of this bottell: Lo here my very and sole Helicon. See here my Fountaine Caballine. This is mine onely Enthusiasmos. Here drinking, I deliberate, I discourse, I resolue and conclude. After the conclusion, I laugh, I vvrite, I compose, I drinke.

Ennius, the father of Latine Poets, drinking did write, writing did drinke.

Aeschylus (if you giue credit to Plutarchus in his bankets) did drinke composing, did compose drinking.[1]

This scene is typical of his attitude of jovial Rabelaisian scorn for stuffy pedants. Rabelais is not an author whom Elizabethans frequently mention and Eliot's detailed knowledge of his book is unusual.

Let us now remember the fact that the name of the pedant in *Love's Labour's Lost* is also the name of the pedant in Rabelais. Might not this suggest that Shakespeare knew of and was in sympathy with Eliot's Rabelaisian satire on pedants? And if at the same time he noticed that the name which the French author gave to his ridiculous schoolmaster was also an anagram of the name of the chief of Eliot's victims—John Florio—would not this have given a double edge to "Holofernes"?

It is also extremely curious to find that Eliot actually makes the suggestion in *Ortho-epia Gallica* that the pretensions of the foreigners would form a suitable subject

---

[1] *Ortho-epia Gallica*, sigs. *f* 1, *f* 1 v.; *Parlement of Pratlers*, p. 37. The passage is derived from Rabelais, *Vie de Gargantua et de Pantagruel*, Book III, Prologue de l'auteur.

for a satirical comedy. The speakers are discussing which is the most ancient of all the languages of the world:

The Hebrew then is the first and most ancient of all tongues?

It hath the first and most ancient place among all tongues that haue bene, that are, and which shall be in the world.

There are some for all that which rashly say to the contrary, and a certaine *Goropius* a Phisition of Brabant, in his bookes intituled *Origines Antuerpianæ*, hath bene so bold to write to proue his Flemish to be the most ancient and first borne of tongues.

Tush, tush, sir, the honest gentleman mistakes himselfe in his grosse volumes.

For all that he laboureth to proue it expresly.

O these are Flemish flamflues, the poore man hath lost his labour therein.

There are more besides him who haue written as much as he.

I beleeue as vvell the one as the other.

Their Feuers quartains.

We shall shew them that their flambumbarkin is not of the antiquitie that they pretend, but was ingendered in Babel, and to be nothing but a barbarous hibber-Iybber, corrupted, effeminat and variable in comparison of the Hebrew, whatsoeuer they dare spit to the contrarie.

It is then a very great impudencie in them to vvrite such filthie lies.

If the Commicall *Aristophanes* were aliue, he should haue here a good argument to write a Commedie of their impudencie.[1]

Goropius Becanus of Brabant had indeed written a book with the title *Origines Antwerpianæ* in which he claimed that Flemish was the most ancient of tongues. This was considered a great joke amongst savants for many years and is here used by Eliot as part of his general policy of ridiculing the foreign refugees, many of whom were Flemish.[2] But that he should actually have suggested that a satirical

[1] *Ortho-epia Gallica*, sigs. F 2 v., F 3.
[2] Some of the London teachers of French were of Flemish extraction. See K. Lambley, *The Teaching and Cultivation of the French Language in England during Tudor and Stuart Times*, 1920, p. 115.

comedy, resembling those of Aristophanes, might be written on such a subject is very strange.

Still more strange is it to recall after this that angry remark of Florio's in the preface to his 1598 dictionary.

> *Let* Aristophanes *and his comedians make plaies, and scowre their mouthes on* Socrates; *those very mouthes they make to vilifie, shall be the meanes to amplifie his vertue.*

These words now suggest to me that, although the "H. S." of the dictionary preface was Hugh Sanford, Florio was here thinking of two other people who had held him up to ridicule, namely Eliot and Shakespeare. This would tally with Warburton's original suggestion, for he never made the statement that "H. S." is Shakespeare. What he did say was that here, in this sentence about Aristophanes and his comedians, Shakespeare is so plainly marked out as not to be mistaken. Perhaps Warburton ought to be excepted from the general remark that none of those who have theorised in the past about Florio and Shakespeare have known of the existence of Eliot's satire. It is possible that Warburton, the first of such theorisers, had reasons which he did not deign to mention for making his assertion that Florio *is* Holofernes.

*   *   *   *

I suggest, therefore, that the case for the presence of satire on Florio in *Love's Labour's Lost* has been very greatly strengthened. The state of affairs in the Southampton *entourage*, as now revealed, is no bar to it, and the evidence of Eliot, and to a lesser extent of Vaughan, undoubtedly tends to give an entirely new force and probability to the theories of those who have sought to establish Florio as the "original" of Holofernes.

On the other hand, there is no exact "portrait" of Florio in the play and the original-hunters go too far in attempting to establish one. The pedant of *Love's Labour's Lost* is a typical schoolmaster of the grammar-school variety, an usher who spends his life stuffing Latin into little boys. That was not Florio's character and profession at all. The Italian teacher was a very elegant and exclusive kind of private tutor, admirably qualified to give a smart "finish" to rich young men and to high-born ladies. In some ways, as Acheson thought, the courtly Armado with his fantastic, rather than pedantic, refinements of speech seems more like Florio than does Holofernes. The answer to this riddle lies in the *commedia dell' arte* framework of the comic underplot. Holofernes and Armado are the typical Pedant and Braggart of Italian comedy, and Shakespeare grafted his topical satire onto the rough traditional outline of those masks. And so, although when Holofernes quoted the "Venetia" proverb or imitated some of the Italian teacher's other mannerisms he was meant to remind the audience of Florio, yet he is not an exact portrait of him. There is satire on other people, as well as on Florio, included in him, as we shall shortly see. The Pedant in the abstract contained within him hints at more than one living pedant, and the genius of Shakespeare could not work, even at satire, without creating. Holofernes *is*—Holofernes.

CHAPTER II

Eliot

Although Florio was the chief victim of Eliot's burlesque, a study of his part in it alone does not do justice to the full significance of *Ortho-epia Gallica*. We next have to consider that work as a whole and to decide whether other elements of Eliot's satire are reflected in *Love's Labour's Lost* besides the attack on Florio and his manuals.

Lest the reader should begin to wonder at this point whether too much importance is not being attached to Eliot's obscure French textbook I propose now to mention two passages from other plays which seem to me to demonstrate fairly conclusively that Eliot's book was one which Shakespeare had studied with some care. Once the *Ortho-epia Gallica* is established as a Shakespearean "source" we can return with greater confidence to our search for traces of it in *Love's Labour's Lost*.

The late Dr J. S. Smart who did so much to clarify the question of Shakespeare's education remarked that the best place in England to acquire the foreign tongues was "London itself, with its foreign colonies and foreign teachers, and the influence of fashionable example; and Shakespeare had hardly arrived there when he plunged into the stream of popular study".[1] This would involve a plunge into those popular modern-language textbooks which were then coming out in considerable numbers, of which Florio's two books of dialogues are examples, and which, as a class, were parodied by Eliot.

That Shakespeare knew of the existence of the kind of book which we have called the modern-language dialogue

[1] J. S. Smart, *Shakespeare, Truth and Tradition*, 1928, pp. 165–6.

is indicated by the following well-known description of the conversation of a traveller:

> Now your traveller,
> He and his toothpick at my worship's mess,
> And when my knightly stomach is sufficed,
> Why then I suck my teeth and catechize
> My picked man of countries: "My dear sir,"
> Thus, leaning on mine elbow, I begin,
> "I shall beseech you"—that is question now;
> And then comes answer like an Absey book:
> "O sir," says answer, "at your best command;
> At your employment; at your service, sir:"
> "No, sir," says question, "I, sweet sir, at yours:"
> And so, ere answer knows what question would,
> Saving in dialogue of compliment,
> And talking of the Alps and Apennines,
> The Pyrenean and the river Po,
> It draws toward supper in conclusion so.
> But this is worshipful society,
> And fits the mounting spirit like myself;
> For he is but a bastard to the time
> That doth not smack of observation....[1]

According to the *Oxford Dictionary* an "Absey book" is a corruption of "ABC-book", that is, a primer or horn-book, "an introductory book to any subject, often in catechism or dialogue form". Clearly the kind of "Absey book" of which Shakespeare was here thinking was in dialogue form, representing a conversation between two speakers, "question" and "answer". Now the fashionable primers of introduction to the "tongues" were conducted in dialogue in just this manner. Shakespeare mentions two subjects with which the dialogue was concerned, namely exchange of compliments and descriptions of travel. Both these subjects are eminently characteristic of the modern-

---

[1] *King John*, I. i. 189–208.

language dialogues. Hear Florio on "To speake with a Gentleman":

Wel met my lord.

How doth your lordship?

Very wel, at the commaundement of you, and redy to serue you in any thing that I may.

Verily I yeeld you thanks, make the like account of me.

Wel my lorde, I goe through this streete, and you.

No sir, I go through this other, wil you commaund me any thing, or not?[1]

And again in his later manual:

Giordano. Why do you stand barehedded? you do yourself wrong.

Edward. Pardon me good sir, I doe it for my ease.

Giordano. I pray you be covered, you are too ceremonious.

Edward. I am so well, that me thinks I am in heauen.

Giordano. If you loue me, put on your hat.

Edward. I will doe it to obay you, not for any plesure that I take in it.

Giordano. What? will you rather stand than sit?

Edward. I am very well. Good lord what dainty knacks you haue here?

Giordano. I haue nothing, but a few trifles.[2]

Now hear Eliot, with his tongue in his cheek, duly producing his "dialogue of compliment" which he calls "To salute men":

I am in a pecke of troubles. As you see.

As vvhole as a rotten fish.

I am glad truly to see you in good health.

I thanke you most heartily.

I thanke you with all my soule.

I thanke you a thousand times.

All our good friends are they vvell?

They are all very vvell, vvith all their little barnes and kinred.

---

[1] *First Fruits*, sigs. B 2 v., B 3.   [2] *Second Fruits*, sigs. P 4, Q 1.

If I may do any thing for you commaund me freely.

I thanke you sir. I am yours, I am at your gentle commande-
ment and seruice.

And I at yours truly. Come to the Court, I vvill do you the
greatest credit that I may possibly.

I shall be sprinckled with the Court holy-water, that is to say,
I shall haue a deluge of ceremonies, but as many apes tailes as
dinners and breakefasts.

Emptie tunnes make more noyse then full vessels.

To foolish vvords stopt eares.[1]

Not only the "dialogue of compliment" but also the travel
dialogue was an important feature of the modern-language
manuals. Florio deals at length with this topic in his
Second Fruits, the sixth chapter of which contains "diuers
necessarie, proffitable, ciuill, & prouerbiall precepts for a
trauailour".

Peeter. How long staide your worship in Italie?
Stephan. I remained two yeares there.
Peeter. Is it not sufficient to see all Italie?
Stephan. Enough and enough, both to see the countrie, and
  to learne the language perfectly.[2]

Eliot's third dialogue is called "The Traueller". It contains descriptions of Spain, Italy, France, and a long and
close parody of the account of England which Florio had
given in his *First Fruits*.[3] I quote the following, however,
from another of Eliot's dialogues called "The Painter".
The speakers are examining a map in a painter's shop.

Looke here Cullion! See Asia. Here are Tygris and Euphrates.
See here Quinzay, a Citie so famous amongst the Azians: and
hath xij. thousand stonebridges, vnder which the ships passe with
full saile, & neuer pull downe their masts.

See Affrick! Here is the mountayn of the Moone!

[1] *Ortho-epia Gallica*, sigs. c 3, c 3 v.; *Parlement of Pratlers*, p. 25.
[2] *Second Fruits*, sigs. P 3, P 4.
[3] See *John Florio*, pp. 156–64.

Seest thou the Fennes of Nyle? Lo here the red Sea. Looke vpon the great Caire! On this side is Europe. This top here all white, are the Hyperborean mountains. Here are the Alpes, ouer which we go downe into Italie. There are the Appenines: and here are the Pyrenæan hilles, by which you may go directly into Spaine.[1]

I think there can be no doubt that Shakespeare's "traveller" with his "dialogue of compliment" and his talk of "the Alps and Apennines, the Pyrenean and the river Po" had studied the modern-language manuals. The Countess de Chambrun has already suggested that the passage in question probably alludes to Florio's two primers.[2] I would endorse that but would add that it is an allusion, not only to Florio's books, but to the whole class of modern-language dialogues and that its mocking tone suggests that Shakespeare knew of Eliot's burlesque of them when he wrote this speech.

I find in another play a further indication that the *Ortho-epia Gallica* was a book known to Shakespeare. In the first of his dialogues Eliot explains his method in teaching, which is what he calls the method of "Nature and Art". By "Nature" he appears to mean vocabulary, and by "Art", grammar and syntax. A list of words is "Nature" and these words combined into sentences form "Art". So pleased was Eliot with this rather elementary and curiously named method[3] that he has the words "Naturâ & Arte" on his title-page and he expatiates at length in his preface and in the first dialogue on its merits, pointing out that it is a great improvement on the easy carelessness

---

[1] *Ortho-epia Gallica*, sig. *k*4; *Parlement of Pratlers*, p. 65.

[2] *Giovanni Florio*, 1921, pp. 142–3; *Shakespeare Actor-Poet*, 1927, pp. 118–19.

[3] It was probably suggested by current methods of Latin teaching. John Brinsley compares the "natural" order of words with the "rhetorical" or "artificial" order of Cicero. See Foster Watson, *English Grammar Schools to* 1660, 1908, p. 411.

of the foreign refugee pedagogues whose order in teaching is "only to read some halfe side", that is, one column of a conversation manual, "and to construe it, vvhich is no great matter, and will not stay aboue halfe an hower to make a lecture, so that they do all things by the halfes".[1] He gives examples to illustrate his method: the following is an extract from one such example:

The Method of Nature.	*The Praxis of Art.*
An Angell.	The Angels sinning became Deuils and wicked spirits, enemies to God and men, and by the diuine iustice being cast downe from their glory on high, fell to the deepest pit of Hell. Where God had prepared a place of punishment according to their sinne, and hath set Lucifer, Beelzebub and Astaroth, wicked spirits, princes raigning ouer the other little Diuels, tortured, tormented and chained all togither in eternall and vnquenchable fire.
A Diuell.	
A maligne Spirit.	
The enemie of God.	
The iustice diuine.	
Hell.	
A deepe pit.	
Lucifer.	
Beelzebub.	
Astaroth.	
The Prince of Diuels.	
A spirit.	
One possest with a Diuell.	
A little Diuell.	
A she Diuell.	
Punishment.	
Sinne.	
To fall.	
To racke.	
To lay in chaines.	
To torment.	
To burne.	
Fire eternall.	
Vnquencheable fire.[2]	

[1] *Ortho-epia Gallica*, sig. D 3. See *John Florio*, pp. 150–1.
[2] *Ortho-epia Gallica*, sigs. E 2, E 2 v. In the original the "Praxis of Art" is not parallel to the list of words but follows them, and the parallel column contains the French.

Let us now consider the following conversation between
Sir Andrew Aguecheek and Sir Toby Belch:

Sir Toby.   Pourquoi, my dear knight?
Sir Andrew.   What is "pourquoi"? do or not do? I would
I had bestowed that time in the tongues, that I
have in fencing, dancing and bear-baiting: O,
had I but followed the arts!
Sir Toby.   Then hadst thou had an excellent head of hair.
Sir Andrew.   Why, would that have mended my hair?
Sir Toby.   Past question; for thou seest it will not curl by
nature.[1]

The mention of the "tongues" and of learning French
leads on immediately to a joke about "nature" and "art".
Whether or not this was meant to be a definite allusion to
Eliot's book which the audience would understand, I think
there can be little doubt that, since learning French was
associated in Shakespeare's mind with "nature" and "art",
he had at some time or another himself read and studied it.

I believe that when the *Ortho-epia Gallica* becomes
better known further curious points of this kind will be
detected, but in the meantime these two passages must
suffice, and I hope that the reader will now return with
a feeling of greater confidence to the examination of *Love's
Labour's Lost* for other traces of Eliot besides the indications of a certain similarity between his and Shakespeare's
attitude to Florio which we collected in the last chapter.

The study of Eliot can illuminate the whole stratum
of allusion to schoolmasters and to textbooks generally
which, as we saw in the introduction, is undoubtedly one
of the layers of topicality in the play.

Eliot's dialogues were a burlesque, not only of modern-
language dialogues, but also of the Latin dialogues or
"colloquies" then generally used in schools to teach boys
to *speak* Latin. He had particularly in mind the Spanish

---

[1] *Twelfth Night*, I. iii. 92–102.

educationalist, Juan Luis Vives, whom he mentions by name in his preface and whose *colloquia*, or *Linguae Latinae Exercitatio* he parodies (particularly in the "Drunken Mens Banket" and in the "Conclusion of the Parlement of Pratlers") as closely as he does Florio's Italian-English dialogues.[1]

Now Shakespeare was also thinking of the Latin colloquies during some of the conversations of his comic pedants in *Love's Labour's Lost*.

Sir Nathaniel. Laus Deo, bone intelligo.
Holofernes. Bone?—bon fort bon!—Priscian a little scratched—'twill serve.
Sir Nathaniel. Videsne quis venit?
Holofernes. Video, et gaudeo.

Professor Dover Wilson regards this as a parody of the Latin colloquies, as has already been recalled.[2] The examples of that class of book which have been most often suggested as possibly in Shakespeare's mind are the *Sententiae pueriles* and *Pueriles confabulatiunculae*.

Here, then, for the second time we find Shakespeare hinting at something which Eliot's parody had recently made *topical*. To laugh at Florio's modern-language dialogues was topical, after Eliot had done so. To laugh at Latin colloquies was also topical, after Eliot's parody of Vives. And since Vives was certainly one of Eliot's victims, might we not take a hint from that and look for traces of Vives in *Love's Labour's Lost*?

A reading of Vive's *Linguae Latinae Exercitatio* with this play in mind produces the following distinctly curious

[1] Eliot probably singled out Vives amongst the authors of Latin colloquies because the writers of modern-language manuals nearly all, including Florio, imitated the themes of Vives to some extent in their dialogues. Also Italian and French translations of his text seem to have been used, in conjunction with the Latin, by students of the modern tongues. (See *John Florio*, pp. 140–3, 145.) The use of Vives was thus associated with the modern-language teachers.

[2] See Introduction, p. 10.

parallel. In the fifth of the colloquies, on "Reading", the
master is teaching his pupils the five vowels. He tells them
to take their "ABC tablet", that is their horn-book, in
their left hands, and then he says:

> Every one of these signs is called a letter. Of these, five are
> vowels, A, E, I, O, U. They are in the Spanish *oveia* which
> signifies *sheep*. Remember that word![1]

The pedagogue has here given his boys an aid to memory.
If they will remember "oveia", the Spanish word for
sheep, they will never forget which are the five vowels.

Very shortly after the conversation in Latin between
Sir Nathaniel and Holofernes quoted above, the following
"set of wit" occurs between Holofernes and Moth:

Armado [*to Holofernes*]. Monsieur, are you not lettered?
Moth.   Yes yes, he teaches boys the horn-book....
           What is a, b, spelt backward with the horn on his
           head?
Holofernes. Ba, pueritia, with a horn added.
Moth.   Ba! most silly sheep with a horn.... You hear his
           learning.
Holofernes. Quis, quis, thou consonant?
Moth.   The last of the five vowels if "you" repeat them,
           or the fifth if "I."
Holofernes [*with caution*]. I will repeat them, a, e, i,—
Moth.   The sheep! the other two concludes it—o, u![2]

The elementary point of this is, of course, that Moth is
trying to get Holofernes to call himself a sheep. He succeeds easily the first time by luring the pedant into saying
"Ba". He then asks Holofernes to repeat the five vowels.
The commentators have worried somewhat over the second
part of the jest. The point, they think, seems to lie in getting
Holofernes to say "I" to which Moth retorts "U sheep!"

---

[1] Foster Watson, *Tudor School-boy Life*, 1908 (this is an English
translation of Vives's *Linguae Latinae Exercitatio*), pp. 18–19.
   [2] v. i. 44–54.

Now does not Vive's device for memorising the vowels by means of the Spanish word for a sheep suddenly and completely illuminate the second half of Moth's joke? He interrupts the pedant at "I" by saying "the sheep" and adds "the other two *concludes it*,—o, u". Concludes what? The letters which make up the Spanish word for a sheep. So Moth twice inveigles Holofernes into calling himself a sheep, once by getting him to say "Ba" and once by getting him to repeat the five vowels. One may add that it is Armado, the Spaniard, who expresses such delight at this jest. I am convinced that in these sheep jokes about vowels and consonants Shakespeare is recalling Vives.

Admirable though they are there is at times a certain priggishness discernible in the dialogues of Vives. Education can achieve the miracle of transforming a boy from an animal into a man. The Child has been playing with his dog, Ruscio, and the Father, anxious to improve each shining hour, makes the dog an introduction to the subject of going to school.

Father. Is thy Ruscio here an animal or a man?

Boy. An animal, as I think.

Father. What have you in you, why you should be a man and not he? You eat, drink, sleep, walk, run, play. So he does all these things also.

Boy. But I am a man.

Father. How do you know this? What have you now, more than a dog? But there is this difference that he cannot become a man. You can, if you will.

Boy. I beg of you, my father, bring this about as soon as possible.

Father. It will be done if you go where animals go, to come back men.

Boy. I will go, father, with all the pleasure in the world! But where is it?

Father. In the school.[1]

[1] *Tudor School-boy Life*, pp. 7–8.

With these elevating remarks ringing in our ears let us now turn to Sir Nathaniel's description of Dull:

> Sir, he hath never fed of the dainties that are bred in a book.
> He hath not eat paper, as it were; he hath not drunk ink:
> His intellect is not replenished, he is only an animal, only sensible in the duller parts:
> And such barren plants are set before us, that we thankful should be,
> Which we of taste and feeling are, for those parts that do fructify in us more than he.[1]

Perhaps Sir Nathaniel was remembering his Vives here though this parallel, if it can be called that, is not so conclusive as is the joke about vowels and sheep. Certain other observations might be made in connection with Vives's strong views on temperance and the dulling effect on the mind of excessive eating and drinking (rudely contradicted by Eliot in his "Drunken Mens Banket") and the quotation of the proverb *Satis quod sufficit* after the meal of which Holofernes has just partaken at the house of a pupil. But a lean and starveling look is an adjunct of the Italian mask of the pedant and one cannot build too much upon that argument.

Having finished with Eliot's burlesque of Latin dialogues we now return to his burlesque of modern-language dialogues, the scope of which was not fully explored in the last chapter in which we were dealing with Florio alone.

Florio was not the only foreign teacher ridiculed by Eliot and his were not the only modern-language manuals which the latter parodied. *The French Alphabet* by G. De la Mothe is a book of French-English dialogues which comes in for a share of Eliot's mockery.[2] De la Mothe was another of the Protestant refugee language-teachers settled in London, and the striking thing about him from our point of view is his name. Does it not remind us of

[1] IV. ii. 24–9.   [2] *John Florio*, pp. 152, 155.

the page "Moth" who associates so much with Armado and with Holofernes in the play? Moth's name was pronounced in the French manner for it gives rise to a pun on "Moth" and "mote".[1] The suggestion has been made that Shakespeare might have taken this name from that of a French ambassador called La Mothe-Fénelon who was in London from 1568 to 1575.[2] But surely a more recent and more obvious source for the name would be this French Protestant refugee teacher called De la Mothe, one of that class of persons at whom Eliot's recent mockery had been directed?

There were numerous other French teachers in London, notably Claudius Hollyband whose dialogues are also parodied by Eliot. A book of Spanish dialogues by one William Stepney is also glanced at in *Ortho-epia Gallica*. Many of the refugees were of Flemish origin and the Flemings are referred to by Eliot with dislike.[3] I suggest that Eliot's anti-alien burlesque provides a kind of key to the strange mingle-mangle of tongues in *Love's Labour's Lost* where scraps of Latin colloquy are jostled by scraps of French and Italian, where Armado once breaks into Spanish[4] and where Katharine mocks the bad Flemish accent.[5] Shakespeare's pedant with the Rabelaisian name and Eliot's Rabelaisian jest at pedants are two halves of a circle which, when joined together, imprison for our inspection some of the people at whom *Love's Labour's Lost* was directed.

Now can all this help at all towards a solution of the central mystery of the scholastic side of the play's reference, namely the "charge-house" allusion?

It is perfectly clear that the "charge-house" was a school of some kind, a place where youth was educated, but beyond that nothing is clear.

---

[1] IV. iii. 158.
[2] Sir Sidney Lee, *Gentleman's Magazine*, October 1880, p. 448.
[3] See p. 47. [4] V. ii. 528.
[5] "'Veal' quoth the Dutchman." V. ii. 247.

There were several schools in London at that time, of a kind which has never been thought of in connection with the "charge-house". Some of the Protestant refugees, instead of becoming private tutors like Florio, opened schools at which they taught French, Latin and other subjects for a fee of so much a week per pupil. The owners of these, perhaps the first "private" schools in England, were mostly Frenchmen. Claudius Hollyband ran a flourishing school and so did De la Mothe and others who are mentioned in Miss Lambley's book on the history of French teaching in England. Eliot's *Ortho-epia Gallica* was directed, not only at the manuals written by the foreign teachers but at the foreign teachers themselves, their methods, their schools, and their anxiety for fees. One of his prefaces is addressed "To the learned professors of the French tongue, in the famous citie of London." The French schoolmasters are therein banteringly accused of having deserted their country to avoid the wars raging there and in order to live comfortably in London where they think of nothing but how to make as much money as possible out of their schools. The Elizabethan was not quite used to the idea of an unendowed school run for private profit. The money made by the French teachers is a sore point with Eliot. "But I must know how much you take by the weeke, by the moneth, by the quarter, by the yeare" asks the pupil of his master in Eliot's second dialogue, imitating similar enquiries made in Hollyband's dialogues, and the lofty reply is:

I make no merchandizing with those whom I teach, for the gifts of the graces and the noble and vertuous qualities ought not to be set on sale.[1]

At the end of the mocking address to the French professors the "gentle doctors of Gaule" are described as spending most of their time in "telling crownes and bags of coyne".

[1] *Ortho-epia Gallica*, sigs. H 3 v., H 4.

Now is it not possible that these French schools in which the charging of fees was such a noticeable feature were called "charge-houses" and that it is to them that Armado's "back-chat" refers?

When a French refugee schoolmaster published a book of French-English dialogues, of the type burlesqued by Eliot, he frequently advertised his school therein by introducing his address into the dialogue. Thus in Peter Du Ploich's *Treatise in English and Frenche* (c. 1553), we find:

> Where goe you to schoole?
> In Trinitie lane, at the signe of the Rose....
> How call you your maister?
> He is called P.

and in Hollyband's *French Littelton* (1576):

In Paules church yard, at the signe of the golden bell: there is a Frenchman, who teacheth both the tongues: that is the Latin, and French: and which doth his dutie.

De la Mothe gives his address in a special paragraph printed on a page to itself just before his dialogues begin. Thus:

An aduertisement to *the Reader*.

Gentle Readers, if there be any of you, that for your better furtherance in the French toung, shal be desirous to be acquainted with the Authour of this booke, you shall heare of him in Fleetstreet beaneth c(o)nduit, at the signe of S. Iohn the Euangelist, vvhere this booke is to be solde: or els in Paules Churchyard at the signe of the Helmet, and there you shall finde him very vvilling to shevv you any fauour and curtesie he may: and most ready to endeuour himselfe to satisfie you, in all that can be possible for him to doe. And thus Fare you vvell.[1]

Does not Armado take special care to elicit the address of Holofernes's school, on the top of the mountain or "mons" the hill?

---

[1] Taken from the 1595 edition of *The French Alphabet*, published by Edward Alde. No copy of Richard Field's edition of 1592 has survived. See Lambley, *op. cit.* p. 162.

The "addresses" of these French schools were generally given by reference to the sign of the nearest bookseller. The chief booksellers lived in St Paul's Churchyard and they "generally seem to have cultivated friendly relations with French teachers, especially those whose books they were commissioned to sell. Frequently they acted as agents for the teachers, who in their grammars advise prospective pupils to 'inquire' at the bookseller's. And, at this time, when indications of address were given by reference to the nearest place of importance, printers' signs are frequently used to locate the situation of French schools."[1] Hollyband, for instance, opened his first school at the "sign of Lucrece", the shop of the printer Thomas Purfoote; De la Mothe taught at the "sign of the Helmet", the address of the bookseller Thomas Chard.

It is to be remarked that Holofernes, who may have been an Italian when quoting the "Venetia" proverb, seems to have been a Frenchman while holding this conversation with Armado. It begins by Armado addressing Holofernes thus:

> Monsieur, are you not lettered?[2]

Armado was supposed to be a Spaniard; why does he say "monsieur" rather than "señor"? "I do sans question", says Holofernes replying to Armado's enquiry whether he does not educate youth at the charge-house on the top of the mountain. Both Quarto and Folio print "sans question" in italics,[3] suggesting that this is not a case of "sans" being used as an English word but that "question" and "sans" were both intended to be taken as French. "Mais oui, sans question," was in effect the reply of Holofernes, indicating his nationality. It has been suggested that the play on "mons" and "mountain" is an allusion to Florio's translation of Montaigne. Though this is not impossible,

[1] Lambley, *op. cit.* p. 129.   [2] v. i. 44.
[3] *sans question.*

chronologically speaking, since Florio was well on with the translation by 1598[1] and may have been known to have been engaged on it earlier, I do not think that it is sound. There are gaps in our knowledge of his career but, so far as is known at present, Florio never kept a school. Certainly he never advertised one in his dialogues, as the French teachers did. I therefore think that the "charge-house" joke was an allusion to one of the French schoolmasters, and not to Florio. Thus explained, the joke fits exactly into the scene in which it occurs—the one which contains the scrap of Latin colloquy and the sheep and vowels pun— for it would be still another reminder of Eliot's parody of the dialogues of the foreign teachers and of Vives, their model.

This interpretation of the "charge-house" allusion is rather a suggestion of the direction in which it might be profitable to look for further evidence than a complete explanation. Was there some actual French school near a printer's sign in which "mons" or "mountain" featured prominently? There is room here for more research into the French schools and their printers' shop addresses. On the other hand, the allusion may have been deliberately made unrecognisable when the play was printed, for the authorities would probably have regarded it as dangerous, anti-alien propaganda. And that brings one to another of the mysterious jokes in *Love's Labour's Lost* with which Eliot might be connected.

*　　　*　　　*　　　*

The following undoubtedly topical reference has never been satisfactorily explained:

Moth. Master, will you win your love with a French brawl?
Armado. How meanest thou? brawling in French?[2]

---

[1] *John Florio*, pp. 213–14.
[2] III. i. 8–10.

There is a pun here on the name of a well-known dance, the French "bransle" or "brawl", and "brawl" meaning to quarrel. But the jest is rather pointless as it stands and this is certainly one of the passages in the play in which the original audience saw more than we can see. To what did "brawling in French" refer?

The influx of Protestant refugees of many nationalities into England during these years aroused a great deal of ill-feeling among the London 'prentices who feared that these skilled foreigners would take the bread out of their mouths in many trades and professions. In the spring of 1593, and again in 1596,[1] there were dangerous anti-alien demonstrations and riots in the streets of London. This brawling was not perhaps entirely in French but it was undoubtedly about Frenchmen and other foreigners. Written attacks on the strangers, warning them to leave the country, were posted in the streets and on the walls of the Dutch church. The authorities made every effort to suppress these riots and to find out and punish the authors of the libels. Apparently they suspected Thomas Kyd, the dramatist, in this connection for he was arrested on 12 May 1593, for being guilty of a "libell that concernd the State".[2] His papers were seized but, so far as is known, nothing was proved against him concerning the libel, though another charge of "atheism" was brought against him in defending himself from which he implicated the dead Marlowe.

The spirit of Eliot's *Ortho-epia Gallica* is closely allied to the spirit of these anti-alien agitations. Miss Lambley points out that the teaching of French in England had long been the monopoly of Englishmen and she suggests that Eliot's dialogues were in part a protest at the swamping

[1] *Shakespeare's Hand in the Play of "Sir Thomas More"*, Shakespeare Problems Series, 1923, Introduction by Dr A. W. Pollard, pp. 22–40.

[2] Thomas Kyd, *Works*, ed. Dr F. S. Boas, 1901, Introduction, pp. lxvi–lxix.

of the modern-language teaching profession by foreign refugees.[1] Thus regarded, the mocking *Ortho-epia* and the brawling London 'prentices are seen to be two expressions of the same feeling.

One wonders, indeed, whether the suspicion of the government ever fell upon Eliot in connection with the anti-alien libels the authors of which they were so anxious to trace. The address to the readers of *Ortho-epia Gallica* is dated 18 April 1593. The anonymous libels were published in May of the same year. One of them begins as follows:

Doth not the World see, that you, beastly Brutes, the *Belgians*, or rather Drunken Drones, and faint-hearted *Flemings*; and you, fraudulent *Father, Frenchmen*, by your cowardly Flight from your own natural Countries, have abandoned the same into the Hands of your proud, cowardly Enemies, and have by a feigned Hypocrisy, and counterfeit shew of Religion, placed yourselves in a most fertile Soil, under a most gracious and merciful Prince. Who hath been contented, to the great Prejudice of her own natural Subjects, to suffer you to live here in better Case and more Freedom, than her own People.[2]

It was in very much this tone of voice that Eliot had in April addressed "the learned professors of the French tongue, in the famous citie of London". The professors are reproached for caring nothing for the misfortunes of their native country which they have abandoned as long as they can eat and drink—particularly drink—comfortably on their profits in England. This is how Eliot begins his address:

Messires, what newes from Fraunce, can you tell? Still warres, warres. A heauie hearing truly: yet if you be in good health, haue many schollers, get good store of Crowns, and drinke good wine, I doubt not but you shall do well, & I desire the good God of heauen to continue it so still.[3]

[1] *Op. cit.* pp. 171–8.
[2] *Shakespeare's Hand in...* "*Sir Thomas More*", p. 39.
[3] *Ortho-epia Gallica*, sig. A 3; *Parlement of Pratlers*, p. 19.

These are the very reproaches of the libel, disguised in banter. One feels that if the authorities had read the *Ortho-epia Gallica* carefully they would have had its author arrested and his papers examined. Did it escape their notice because of its innocent disguise as a textbook for students of the French tongue?

Eliot reproaches the French schoolmasters for caring nothing about the "warres, warres" still raging in their own unhappy country so long as they can lead a pleasant and comfortable life in England—such a life as the philosopher Epictetus led,

...who did nothing else all his life time but take his eases, and as a renowned poet sayth in your owne language:

> Saulter, dançer, faire les tours,
> Boire vin blanc & vermeil,
> Et ne rien faire tous les iours,
> Que conter escuz au soleil.[1]
> *Id est,*
> *Skip and dance, trip on toe,*
> *Drinking White and Claret-wine:*
> *And naught euery day did doe,*
> *But tell crownes and bags of coyne.*

I greet you all, gentle doctors of Gaule, *Adieu.*[2]

I suggest that this picture of the French teachers gaily dancing with delight at their good fortune is the origin of the punning in the play on "French brawl" and "brawling in French". This, like that to the "charge-house", would have been a dangerous allusion which those responsible for printing the play would not have wished to leave in too obvious a form.

[1] Eliot had found these verses in Rabelais, Book II, chap. xxx.
[2] *Ortho-epia Gallica*, sig. A 4v; *Parlement of Pratlers*, p. 21. Hollyband's *French Littelton* had contained a treatise on the iniquity of dancing which may have suggested to Eliot the idea of presenting the French professors in the act of cutting capers.

"Warres, warres" in France. And what were the names of some of the leaders in those civil brawls with which France was so distracted? The King of Navarre, the Maréchal Biron, the Duc de Longueville, the Duc de Mayenne. Is it possible that we are here stumbling upon a connection between the "schoolmaster" jokes in *Love's Labour's Lost* and the "French news" atmosphere of the play suggested by the names of the leading characters?

Eliot was a translator of French news-letters for John Wolfe, the printer.[1] All his books are either translations from French or connected in some way with France and the French language. He tells us in the dialogues that he had travelled widely in France and had lived there for some years. He would thus be a very suitable candidate for the rôle of that mysterious "English or French traveller" who, according to Sir Edmund Chambers,[2] probably gave Shakespeare orally the information about events in French history, such as the meeting of Henry of Navarre and Marguerite de Valois at Nérac in 1578, with which the play shows him to have been acquainted, but which he could not have found extant in any printed source at that time. But that would involve us in suggesting that Shakespeare not only knew of the *Ortho-epia Gallica* and its anti-alien significance but also knew its author personally—an assumption which it is perhaps not quite justifiable to make at this stage of the argument.

*　　　*　　　*　　　*

There is one last step to take before leaving this schoolmaster aspect of the problem, and that is to compare *Love's Labour's Lost* with another play of much the same period which is undoubtedly strongly anti-alien in tendency and which is, moreover, particularly directed against the foreign teachers.

---

[1] *John Florio*, pp. 175–7.　　　[2] See Introduction, p. 3.

Henslowe's diary proves that William Haughton's *Englishmen for my Money or a Woman will have her Will*[1] was in existence in 1598, the year in which *Love's Labour's Lost* was published, but it was not printed until 1616. It describes how three "strangers", a Frenchman, a Dutchman and an Italian, are supplanted by three Englishmen in their suit for the daughters of an English merchant. An English schoolmaster of the name of Anthony, who is tutor to the daughters, plays a large part in the intrigue. He is discharged by the girls' father who has overheard him pleading the Englishmen's suit with his pupils whilst supposed to be giving them a lesson in "Morall Philosophy". The father determines to replace him by a French tutor and to trust no longer in a "smooth-fac'd *Englishman*". He instructs his servant to go to "Powles" and engage a French master for his daughters. But Anthony disguises himself, goes to Paul's, accosts the servant there who is looking about for a Frenchman, and by pretending to talk in broken English manages to get himself re-engaged as the new French tutor and is thus able to continue aiding and abetting the plans of the English suitors. What is, I think, significant about this is the kind of language which Anthony uses when he is pretending to be a French teacher:

Anthony. I beseech you *Monsieur*, giue mee audience.
Frisco. What would you haue? What should I giue you?
Anthony. Pardon, sir mine vnciuill and presumptuous intrusion, who indeauour nothing lesse, then to prouoke or exasperat you against mee.
Frisco. They say, a word to the Wise is enough: so by this litle *French* that he speakes, I see hee is the very man I seeke for: Sir, I pray what is your name?
Anthony. I am nominated *Monsieur Le Mouche*, and rest at your *bon* seruice.
Frisco. I vnderstand him partly; yea, and partly nay: Can you speake French? *Content pore vous monsieur Madomo.*

[1] Reprinted by the Malone Society, 1912.

Anthony. If I could not sir, I should ill vnderstand you: you speake the best French that euer trode vpon Shoe of Leather.

Frisco. Nay, I can speake more Languages then that: This is *Italian,* is it not? *Nella slurde Curtezana.*

Anthony. Yes sir, and you speake it like a very Naturall.

Frisco. I beleeue you well: now for *Dutch*: *Ducky de doe watt heb yee ge brought.*

Anthony. I pray you stop your mouth, for I neuer heard such *Dutch* before brocht.

Frisco. Nay I thinke you haue not met with no pezant:[1] Heare you M. *Mouse* (so your name is I take it) I haue considered of your learning in these aforesaid Languages, and find you reasonable: So, so, now this is the matter; Can you take the ease to teach these Tongues to two or three Gentlewomen of mine acquaintance, and I will see you paide for your labour.

Anthony. Yes sir, and that most willingly.[2]

Are not these exaggerated *politesses,* these long words such as "nominate", and "give audience" somewhat in the vein of Holofernes and of Armado?

When one of the daughters is describing to her sisters the manner in which she is wooed by Aluaro, the Italian, she quotes him as talking thus:

> ...hee can tell
> Of Lady *Venus,* and her Sonne blind *Cupid*:
> Of the faire *Scilla* that was lou'd of *Glaucus,*
> And yet scornd *Glaucus,* and yet lou'd King *Minos*;
> Yet *Minos* hated her, and yet she holp'd him;
> And yet he scorn'd her, yet she kild her Father
> To doe her good; yet he could not abide her.[3]

This is a species of "Arcadian rhetoric" which would have appealed to Armado, as well as to Aluaro.

---

[1] I.e. "pedant". [2] Malone Society reprint, ll. 920–49.
[3] *Ed. cit.* ll. 987–93.

Haughton had, I think, undoubtedly read *Ortho-epia Gallica*; and his play is a reflection of feeling against the foreign teachers. And that his foreigners and pretended foreigners should use in speaking affectations not unlike some of those in *Love's Labour's Lost* is a point in favour of the present argument.

*   *   *   *

To summarise shortly the position as it now stands, I would say that the schoolmaster jokes, and possibly some of the "French news" atmosphere in *Love's Labour's Lost* are to be explained as allusions to the anti-alien feeling of those years, and particularly to Eliot's attack on the alien teachers and his parody of their manuals. The fact that many of the hits of this nature in the play are somewhat obscure is to be accounted for by the danger of printing such matter in any easily recognisable form. The evidence is somewhat scattered and many of the points are perhaps unimportant when viewed apart from the general argument, but on the whole the case seems to me already fairly convincing. The really convincing part of it is, however, yet to come. For by far the most striking feature of this Eliot-Florio clue is the way in which it will be found to fit in with other aspects of the play's satire.

CHAPTER III

Harvey and Nashe

Eliot and Florio are alluded to more than once in the
writings of Harvey and Nashe. It would seem that Nashe
was on Florio's side over the latter's quarrel with Hugh
Sanford; whilst Eliot, through his association with Wolfe
who was Harvey's printer, may have been technically in
the Harvey camp. I have partially worked out some of
the links between Eliot and Florio and the Harvey-Nashe
controversy in my book on Florio,[1] but there are probably
other allusions there which could be similarly elucidated.
Harvey's as yet unpublished marginal notes in his copies
of Florio's *First Fruits*, Eliot's *Ortho-epia Gallica*, and
other modern-language textbooks might be of importance
in this connection.

Further discoveries may await investigation in this field,
but in the meantime we already know enough to suggest
that the fact that there are undoubted allusions to the
Harvey-Nashe controversy in *Love's Labour's Lost* need
not deter us from our Eliot-Florio theory, since Florio and
Eliot were also mixed up in that controversy.

The pamphlet which is the most closely associated with
Love's Labour's Lost is Gabriel Harvey's *Pierces Supererogation* (1593) from which Shakespeare borrowed the joke
about piercing a hogshead.[2] And it is in that very same
pamphlet that Harvey makes a long allusion to Eliot which
we must now examine with some care.

Harvey is replying to something which Nashe had said
in *Strange Newes*. Nashe there had argued at some length
that experience of life was a better school for authors than

---

[1] *John Florio*, pp. 174-87.　　　[2] See Introduction, p. 4.

an academic education. He was glad, he said, that he had in his time lived somewhat riotously, and had "dealt vpon spare commodities of wine and capons" when imprisoned for debt in the Counter. He takes the Counter (the name of the Elizabethan debtors' prison) as a kind of symbol of "villany" or experience of life and he says that his inspiration as a writer is derived from such experience.

...I protest I should neuer haue writ passion well, or beene a peece of a Poet, if I had not arriu'd in those quarters [i.e. the Counter].[1]

Later he again extols the superiority of the debtors' prison over the universities as a school of wit.

Cambridge and Oxford may stande vnder the elbowe of it.[2]

In *Pierces Supererogation*, Harvey, who was the academic mind personified, tried to answer all this. These roystering youths reared in the school of villainy are, he says, pushing aside us poor old fellows who have been "simply trayned after the Athenian, and Romane guise". We must now say farewell to our dear mothers, the once flourishing universities, for "one sure Conny-catcher" is now worth "twenty Philosophers", and Oxford and Cambridge have become

the slaues of that dominiering eloquence, that knoweth no Art but the cutting Arte; nor acknowledgeth any schoole, but the Curtisan schoole.[3]

He points out that all this "ruffian Rhetorique" and "curtisan Philosophy" is really nothing but "villany"; and "villany" is indeed, according to Harvey, the chief characteristic both of Nashe's character and of his literary style.

This reminds Harvey that he had recently been discussing this very question with someone, and, in the course of the conversation, this friend had delivered an opinion

[1] Thomas Nashe, *Works*, ed. R. B. McKerrow, I, 310.
[2] *Ibid., loc. cit.*   [3] Harvey, *Works*, ed. A. B. Grosart, II, 52.

upon Nashe and upon his style. Harvey then quotes in italics a long speech about Nashe which this anonymous friend had made.

Now this "friend" into whose mouth Harvey puts a long speech about Nashe was undoubtedly John Eliot. The "friend" says that he has recently "shaken so manie learned asses by the eares, as it were by the hands", and Eliot at the end of one of his *Ortho-epia Gallica* prefaces had said "I will be breefe, and shake you straight by the hands, but because here are three or foure asses, I shall shake them first by the eares". The "asses" who were to be shaken by the ears were, of course, the manual-writers whose dialogues Eliot intended to parody. Eliot's preface is dated 18 April 1593; Harvey's *Pierces Supererogation* is dated 27 April, that is only nine days later. Both publications emanated from Wolfe's press. Moreover, there are numerous other points of style and subject-matter about the speech by which it can be connected with Eliot which it is unnecessary to repeat here because they have already been set forth elsewhere[1]. There can be no doubt that this "friend" is meant to be Eliot, and that being so we can now proceed to see what, according to Harvey were Eliot's views on Nashe.[2]

Eliot strongly endorses Nashe's own view that experience of life, even if it be of "villany", is a better school for writers than an academic training or much book-learning. The whole speech is really nothing but this argument expressed in various ways. Nashe would never, says Eliot, have written that famous work *Pierce Penilesse* if he had not been "deeply plunged in a profound exstasie of knauery". Such work is truly great and original, and until he sees anything as good as this coming from an academic pen Eliot will continue to prefer "one smart Pamflet or knauery" before "ten blundring volumes of the nine

[1] *John Florio*, pp. 178–83.
[2] The speech is reprinted in full in Appendix I, pp. 203–5.

Muses". Life is a strange dream, full of smoke and noise;
it is like a comedy or a tragedy, and the stirring wit of man
is a quintessence of quicksilver, impossible to hold down
within narrow limits. The natural, sanguine, wit should
be encouraged and not cramped with art and artifice.
"One good fellow with his odd iestes, or one madd knaue
with his awke hibber-gibber, is able to putt downe twentye
of your smuggest artificiall men, that simper it so nicely,
and coylie in their curious pointes." The Elizabethan
used "art" and "artificial" in the sense of "learning" and
"learned". Eliot is all for "Sanguine witt" as opposed
to "Melancholy Arte". It is his native invention which
makes Nashe so readable, and those modern young men
who wish to write works as good as, or better than, his
should follow his example and learn in the school of life,
leaving it to others to "closely sitt" or "sokingly ly" at
their books in order to purchase with great sums of study
and candles "the worshipfull names of Dunses, & Dodipoles". The best modern writers are those who have
understood, like Nashe, the secret of life, or "villany".
It is the "multiplying spirit", not of the learned alchemist,
but of the lively "villanist" which knocks the nail on the
head and gets farther in a day than will the quickest
"artist" in a week. Eliot therefore urges his "good
frends" who love "the sweete world" to follow Nashe's
advice, learn from life, and so achieve the advancement of
their "commendable partes". All is nothing without advancement, and, in the modern world, the "villanist" will
make good before the "artist". At the conclusion of his
speech Eliot alludes to those artificial "asses" (Florio and
the others) whom he has recently "shaken by the ears",
or parodied in his recent dialogues, and Harvey winds up
the whole episode by adding, after the speech, that it was
Eliot's use of the word "supererogation" to describe Nashe's
Pierce Penilesse which gave him the idea of entitling his
reply to that pamphlet *Pierces Supererogation*.

If for "villany"—the term which Eliot and Nashe use to cover direct experience of life[1]—we substitute the word "love', which in Berowne's vocabulary denotes direct experience through living, the argument of Eliot's speech is immediately seen to be much the same as the argument of *Love's Labour's Lost*. "I prefer one smart Pamflet of knauery, before ten blundring volumes of the nine Muses." "You that purpose with great summes of studdy, & candles to purchase the worshipfull names of Dunses, & Dodipoles, may closely sitt, or sokingly ly at your bookes...."

> Why, all delights are vain, but that most vain
> Which, with pain purchased, doth inherit pain—
> As painfully to pore upon a book....[2]
> Small have continual plodders ever won,
> Save base authority from others' books....[3]
> Why, universal plodding prisons up
> The nimble spirits in the arteries....[4]

"It is the Multiplying spirit, not of the Alchimist, but of the villanist, that knocketh the naile one the head, and spurreth cutt farther in a day, then the quickest Artist in a weeke."

> Other slow arts entirely keep the brain;
> And therefore, finding barren practisers,
> Scarce show a harvest of their heavy toil.
> But love, first learnéd in a lady's eyes,
> Lives not alone immuréd in the brain;
> But with the motion of all elements,
> Courses as swift as thought in every power,
> And gives to every power a double power,
> Above their functions and their offices.[5]

[1] Eliot and Nashe are not really using the word "villainy" otherwise than in its usually accepted sense, but their talk of "villainy" is a serio-comic exaggeration. They are contrasting the man of strong natural wit, judgment and common sense who forms himself in the school of life (the "villanist") with the man of weak judgment and much ill-assimilated learning (the "artist"). The whole problem is admirably thrashed out by Montaigne in his essay "Of Pedantisme" (Book I, chapter XXIV).   [2] I. i. 72–4.
[3] I. i. 86–7.   [4] IV. iii. 301–2.   [5] IV. iii. 321–9.

"Art", which started in such high favour at the beginning
of the play,

> Our court shall be a little academe,
> Still and contemplative in living art,[1]

is thoroughly discredited and overwhelmed by life, in the
shape of the ladies and the love which they bring. And this
love stimulates the mental powers of the would-be "artists"
in a way undreamed of before its advent.

> Never durst poet touch a pen to write,
> Until his ink were temp'red with Love's sighs;
> O, then his lines would ravish savage ears,
> And plant in tyrants mild humility.
> From women's eyes this doctrine I derive:
> They sparkle still the right Promethean fire—
> They are the books, the arts, the academes,
> That show, contain, and nourish all the world.[2]

Has not "Sanguine witt" completely vanquished "Melancholy Arte"? And are not the smug "artificiall men, that
simper it so nicely, and coylie in their curious pointes"
(how admirable this is as a description of Holofernes and
Armado!) most thoroughly "putt downe" before the play
is over? Berowne's are the arguments of Harvey's anonymous friend transposed by genius from a local to a universal
application, transmuted from satire into poetry.

When we remember that it was from *Pierces Supererogation* that Shakespeare borrowed the "piercing a hogshead"
joke for *Love's Labour's Lost* it is somewhat impressive
to find, also in *Pierces Supererogation*, this speech attributed
to Eliot the theme of which is essentially the same as the
theme of Shakespeare's comedy.

How much are we justified in deducing from this? Can
we begin to think at this point that Eliot was someone

---

[1] I. i. 13–14.   [2] IV. iii. 343–50.

whom Shakespeare knew personally? Let us now listen once again to the speech of the Bastard in *King John*:

> Now your traveller,
> He and his toothpick at my worship's mess,
> And when my knightly stomach is sufficed,
> Why then I suck my teeth and catechize
> My picked man of countries: "My dear sir,"
> Thus, leaning on mine elbow, I begin,
> "I shall beseech you"—that *is* question now;
> And then comes answer like an Absey book:
> "O sir," says answer, "at your best command;
> At your employment; at your service, sir:"
> "No, sir," says question, "I, sweet sir, at yours:"
> And so, ere answer knows what question would,
> Saving in dialogue of compliment,
> And talking of the Alps and Apennines,
> The Pyrenean and the river Po,
> It draws toward supper in conclusion so.
> But this is worshipful society,
> *And fits the mounting spirit like myself;*
> *For he is but a bastard to the time*
> *That doth not smack of observation....*

The first part of this is, as we have already said, a fairly clear allusion to the modern-language manuals and to Eliot's mocking parody of their "dialogues of compliment" and "travel dialogues". And are not the sentiments expressed in the last three lines the same as those which we have just been examining in the Eliot speech quoted by Harvey? "Mounting spirits" like himself, says the Bastard, must move amongst people and "smack of observation" for this is the way to move with the times and to rise in the modern world. It is the "multiplying spirit" of "villany", or experience of the world, says Eliot, which is the "Archmistery of the busiest Modernistes" and the secret of success which he recommends to his friends, for, "all is nothing without aduancement". Coming immediately after the allusion to Eliot's parody of the dialogues this kind of talk seems to me also to recall Eliot's point of view and to suggest that the author of *Ortho-epia Gallica* had, at some time or another, expounded his views in Shakespeare's hearing.

* * * *

Since this speech of Eliot's seems to take the same side in the controversy between "artists" and "villanists" as does Shakespeare in *Love's Labour's Lost*, it might be a helpful guide to the satire in the play. We know what people Eliot had in mind in that speech. Might they not be the same people whom Shakespeare had in mind in his play?

In his speech against "artists" Eliot was thinking

(1) of Florio and the writers of modern-language manuals whom he had recently "shaken by the ears" in his *Ortho-epia Gallica*;

(2) of Harvey with whom he was talking and against whom he was defending the sprightly "villany" of Nashe.

Our first two chapters were devoted to arguing that the first of these *is* reflected in *Love's Labour's Lost*. And as to the second, have not many people maintained with a great deal of reason, that Holofernes and Armado have much in common with the pedantic Harvey? I suggest that both these views are right. Neither Florio nor Harvey are "originals" of Holofernes or of Armado, but when Shakespeare elaborated his typical pedant and his typical braggart he was thinking of various "artists" who were known to him (and to Eliot). Harvey was one of these; Florio, and probably some of the other foreign teachers were others. Holofernes and Armado glance maliciously through their masks now at Florio and the modern-language teachers, and now at Gabriel Harvey.

Rather a curious feature of the whole situation is that although Eliot's sympathies were obviously with Nashe, he was technically on Harvey's side, as already noted. He belonged to the Wolfe camp and Harvey introduces him as his "friend" into *Pierces Supererogation*.

I am not sure that this anomaly is not reflected in the position of Moth, who is so much like Nashe, in *Love's Labour's Lost*. Moth is there technically allied to the pedants and "arts-men", just as Nashe was allied to Florio, and yet he is not quite "of" them, just as Nashe really had more in common with Eliot than with Florio. He laughs at Armado and Holofernes behind their backs. His precocious wit is viewed with indulgence. He is voluble and natural, rather than artificial, in his discourse. It is not impossible that Moth's indeterminate position in *Love's Labour's Lost* reflects some actual situation, which we are dimly beginning to perceive, amongst persons who were well known to Shakespeare and to his audience.

The issue between Eliot and Florio is thus linked to the issue between Nashe and Harvey. Florio and Harvey are both "artists", believers in book-learning and in a consciously elaborate style of speaking and writing. Eliot and Nashe are "natural" or "sanguine" wits. This was the issue which Shakespeare had under consideration in *Love's Labour's Lost*, and he is on the side of the sanguine wits, like Berowne, and against the artists, like Holofernes and Armado. Therefore it is highly probable that there are traces of hits at Harvey, as well as at Florio, in the discourses of Armado and Holofernes. It is impossible to repeat here all the theories relating to Harvey's presence in the play, but one point which has been made by Harvey enthusiasts should be noted. Nashe objected to Harvey calling him "as deeplie learned, as *Fauste precor gelida*", the opening line of the eclogues of Mantuan which he regarded as typical of the "Grammar-Schoole witte".[1] It is this very line from Mantuan which Holofernes quotes,

[1] See H. C. Hart's note to IV. ii. 87–8 in the Arden edition of *Love's Labour's Lost*.

or rather misquotes, at the beginning of the speech which contains the "Venetia" proverb. There is surely an echo of the Harvey-Nashe controversy here. Holofernes, the "arts-man", quotes the tag which Nashe and Harvey both thought typical of a grammar-school wit, of an "artist". And then he goes on to quote an Italian tag typical of another "arts-man", John Florio. This seems to bring us very close to Eliot's speech against "artists" in which we know that he was thinking (1) of Harvey and Nashe, and (2) of the artificial "asses", of whom Florio was the chief, whose dialogues he had parodied. Therefore the arguments of those who have thought that Harvey was the "original" of Holofernes are not entirely misleading. The satire on pedantry and artificiality in *Love's Labour's Lost* is broad enough to include both Florio and Harvey, and as we have seen that Florio, Eliot, Harvey and Nashe were all inextricably entangled with one another, there can be little doubt that it does include them both.

*   *   *   *

Harvey and Nashe have thus not discouraged us from our convictions. By repeating Eliot's speech on "artists" and "villanists" Harvey has shown us that Eliot and Shakespeare saw eye to eye in this matter. And by indicating that Eliot thought of Harvey, as well as of Florio, as an "artist", the speech in *Pierces Supererogation* has demonstrated that the Harvey-Nashe echoes in *Love's Labour's Lost* chime perfectly naturally with the Eliot-Florio echoes.

CHAPTER IV

Chapman

We now reach a phase in the development of this argument which always seems to me highly significant. One of the best established facts about the satire in *Love's Labour's Lost* is that it had something to do with Raleigh and his friends and with the expression of their point of view which George Chapman put forward in his poem *The Shadow of Night* (1594).[1] And it is my belief that in his dedication to that work Chapman is deliberately answering the arguments of the Eliot speech in *Pierces Supererogation*.

In the following quotation from Chapman's famous address to Royden I have italicised two words:

> How then may a man stay his maruailing to see passion-driuen men, reading but to curtoll a tedious houre, and altogether hidebownd with affection to great mens fancies, take vpon them as killing censures as if they were iudgements Butchers, or as if the life of truth lay tottering in their verdits.
>
> Now what a *supererogation* in wit this is, to thinke skil so mightilie *pierst* with their loues, that she should prostitutely shew them her secrets, when she will scarcely be lookt vpon by others but with invocation, fasting, watching; yea not without hauing drops of their soules like an heauenly familiar.[2]

Why drag in "pierst" in connection with "supererogation" in this clumsy way unless as an allusion to the title of Harvey's pamphlet, published the year before? And Harvey says that it was Eliot's remarks about Nashe which made him think of giving his book that title. Further, Chapman is complaining of people who imagine that they

---

[1] See Introduction, pp. 5–9.
[2] The whole dedication is reprinted in Appendix II, pp. 205–6.

can dispense with industrious application, who hope to acquire "skil" by the light of nature without undergoing the hard intellectual discipline through which others pursue it. Harvey would agree with Chapman in such disapproval, and indeed argues from that point of view in *Pierces Supererogation*, *except* when he stands aside and allows Eliot to put forward the claims of the "villanist" as against the "artist". Therefore Chapman is not here answering *Pierces Supererogation* as a whole, but only the Eliot speech in it.

In his next sentence Chapman speaks with disdain of the pursuit of worldly advancement by these "profit-rauisht" wits who neglect serious study. Had not Eliot adjured his "villanist" friends to look well to their worldly careers? "O my good frends, as ye loue the sweete world, or tender your deare selues, be not vnmindfull what is good for the aduauncemente of your commendable partes." I ask the reader to turn now to the end of this book and to read through the Eliot speech and the Chapman dedication. I think he will be convinced that there is undoubtedly a connection between them.

The significance of this is that many people have very strongly suspected that Chapman's talk here about passion-driven men, hidebound with affection to great men's fancies, who think that they can pierce skill to the heart by their natural wits, who read only to curtail a tedious hour, and who are anxious to make money, refers, somewhat jealously, to Shakespeare's success as a poet and a dramatist and to his friendship with the Earl of Southampton. If that is true, and if it is also true that the dedication is a reply to the Eliot speech in *Pierces Supererogation*, then Chapman practically tells us that when Eliot talks in that speech about those friends of his whom he advises to be "villanists", like Nashe, so that they may advance their commendable parts, he is talking about none other than Shakespeare himself, that Shakespeare was a "mounting spirit" whom he advised to "smack of observation".

Thus Chapman would confirm our whole thesis for us
For if Shakespeare is one of the "villanists" in the Eliot
speech, then we are quite right in thinking that Eliot and
Shakespeare at this time were looking at contemporary
controversies and contemporary persons from a similar angle.
This strongly encourages us to continue searching in the
Eliot speech for clues to the satire of *Love's Labour's Lost.*

That Chapman felt it incumbent upon him to reply to
that speech suggests that he had taken to himself some of
Eliot's slighting remarks about "artists". And, now one
comes to think of it, certain phrases in the speech, such
as that about the "multiplying spirit" of alchemists, or
the "quintessence of quicksilver", might indicate scientific
studies of the kind congenial to Chapman and his friends.
The names and authors which Eliot mentions, only to
dismiss them as well enough for smug artificial men but
a waste of time for good fellows who have better things
to do, also tend to recall the interests of Chapman and of
the Raleigh group generally.

You may discourse of Hermes ascending spirit; of Orpheus
enchanting harpe; of Homers diuine furie; of Tyrtaeus enraging
trumpet; of Pericles bounsinge thunderclaps; of Platos enthusiasticall rauishment; and I wott not what maruelous egges in mooneshine: but a fly for all your flying speculations, when one good
fellow with his odd iestes, or one madd knaue with the awke hibber-
gibber, is able to putt downe twentye of your smuggest artificiall
men, that simper it so nicely, and coylie in their curious pointes.

Hermes is not only the mercurial messenger god but also
the Egyptian Hermes Trismegistus after whom the Her-
metic philosophy was named. He was always associated
with the study of alchemy, and Peele mentions "Trismegistus" and Pythagoras as being the intellectual guides of
the Earl of Northumberland, who was a noted member of
the "School of Night". After "Hermes ascending spirit"
Eliot mentions "Orpheus enchanting harpe". Chapman's
Shadow of Night owes a great deal to the Orphic literature

of the third and fourth centuries. As to "Homers diuine furie" it is possible that Chapman had begun his great translation, or at least had displayed an interest in Homer, as early as this. I do not know that Tyrtaeus or Pericles were particularly affected by the "School of Night", but Plato was enthusiastically studied by them all. The "villanist", as advised by Eliot, is not to study authors like these but to inure his "mercuriall fingers" (again this alchemical play on mercury or quicksilver) to frame works of supererogation which shall be based on life itself, like Nashe's *Pierce Penilesse*.

These hints, and above all the fact that Chapman replied to them, indicate that Eliot included Chapman and the "School of Night" among his "artists". We now have, therefore, the complete list of the people of whom Eliot was thinking in that speech. They were:

(1) Florio and the modern-language manual writers, since he refers to having recently "shaken asses by the ears".

(2) Harvey, for he is discussing Nashe's "villanist" style which he prefers to a more learned manner.

(3) Chapman and the "School of Night", for Chapman replied to this speech.

Therefore Chapman may join Florio and Harvey as the third of the "artists" of whom Shakespeare was thinking when he constructed his mask-like figures of Holofernes and Armado.

*   *   *   *

The impudent wit of Moth (Nashe) in the play can now be better understood. His mockery of Holofernes and Armado is the laughing contempt of a "villanist" for "artists".

Armado. I have promised to study three years with the duke.
Moth. You may do it in an hour, sir.
Armado. Impossible.
Moth. How many is one thrice told?

Armado. I am ill at reck'ning, it fitteth the spirit of a tapster.
Moth.   You are a gentleman and a gamester, sir.
Armado. I confess both—they are both the varnish of a complete man.
Moth.   Then I am sure you know how much the gross sum of deuce-ace amounts to.
Armado. It doth amount to one more than two.
Moth.   Which the base vulgar do call three.
Armado. True.
Moth.   Why sir, is this such a piece of study? Now here is three studied ere ye'll thrice wink: and how easy it is to put "years" to the word "three," and study "three years" in two words, the dancing horse will tell you.[1]

With his lightning jest Moth runs in a moment through something over which Armado intended to take three years. The mathematical character of these puns suggests that Armado is here representing Chapman for the moment. But when Moth trips up Holofernes over the sheep and vowels riddle,—

Moth. Ba! most silly sheep with a horn.... You hear his learning[2]

it is of the stupidity of schoolmasters, in spite of their learning, that he is thinking. And when Holofernes displays such delight on hearing the "piercing a hogshead" jest, the point about it which strikes him most is that it fell from the lips of that "natural", that "turf of earth" hight Costard:

Holofernes. Master Person—quasi pierce-one? And if one should be pierced, which is the one?
Costard.   Marry, master schoolmaster, he that is likeliest to a hogshead.
Holofernes. Piercing a hogshead! a good lustre of conceit in a turf of earth, fire enough for a flint, pearl enough for a swine: 'tis pretty, it is well.[3]

[1] I. ii. 35–54.   [2] v. i. 48–9.   [3] IV. ii. 87–93.

Again and again it is the "natural" wits who confound the "arts-men" in the play, and the explanation of this lies in the fact that the wit of Shakespeare had been classed with that of Nashe as being of the "villanist" variety which could go farther in a day than the quickest "artist" in a week.

CHAPTER V

Bruno and the "School of Night"

We began with Florio, who led us to Eliot, who led us to Harvey, who led us to Chapman and so to the "School of Night", or Raleigh group, with its scientific and learned preoccupations, satire upon which is generally recognised as being the key to the mystery of *Love's Labour's Lost*. We shall now return to the guide with whom we started—Florio—and explore with him another path. The point of departure now is not Florio's enmity with Eliot, but his friendship with Bruno. If we follow Florio along that road we shall find ourselves arriving a second time, though by another route, at the "School of Night".

The great Italian thinker Giordano Bruno was in England from 1583 to 1586 living in the house of the French ambassador in London, where Florio was also employed. During that time Bruno published several books, in Italian and in dialogue form, in which he expounded his philosophy. As is well known, he was an early believer in the Copernican theory and his life-work was an attempt to construct a philosophy which should cover the new and startling view of the universe and of man's place in it which Copernicus's great discovery had revealed.

The Copernican theory had made very little headway in England at that time and Bruno's ideas were not received with much favour. He was an irritable person and the slow-witted prejudices of English Aristotelians annoyed him intensely. On his arrival in England in 1583 he went first of all to Oxford. He disputed publicly there with some English doctors who, he says, were very rude, ignorant men and quite unworthy of his metal. He is equally contemptuous of the English doctors, Torquato and Nundinio, with whom he disputed concerning the Copernican theory at the supper-party in London which he describes in the *Cena de le ceneri*. They knew more about beer than they did about Greek. They were most stupid and barbarous persons, and it was casting pearls before swine for him to display the treasures of his intellect before them. Most of the so-called educated people whom he met in England had the mentality of a ploughman or a cowherd, and as for their university of Oxford, it is a mere pit of ignorance and barbarism. The English are rough and coarse in their manners, the mobs in their streets are very rude to foreigners and, on the whole, the island is no place for a civilised Italian. It was into this book that Florio was introduced by name as Bruno's friend and upholder. It gave a great deal of offence, and in his next work *De la causa, principio, e uno*, in which Florio also appears as Elitropio, Bruno apologised for his rudeness about England and the English people, and in particular for what he had said about Oxford.

These sensations had taken place eight or nine years before the earliest date at which *Love's Labour's Lost* could have been written. But Florio had more recently re-opened the wound. Into the dialogues of his *Second Fruits*, published in 1591, he introduced Bruno under his well-known name of "Nolano" and also two persons called Torquato and Nundinio whom he characterised by slight but unmistakable touches as being the same as the Torquato and Nundinio of the *Cena*. Moreover, in the course of the dialogues he allowed himself here and there to express a good deal of discontentment with English manners and customs, the uncivilised nature of the drama in England, the heavy feeding of Englishmen, the discomfort of English saddles, and so on. These were small enough pin-pricks in themselves, but coupled with the deliberate inclusion of the names Nolano, Torquato and Nundinio they must have revived the memory of Bruno's rudeness in the *Cena* about English ways, and particularly about English doctors and English universities. Taken in conjunction with the extremely combative tone of his epistle to the reader, signed "Resolute I.F.", these details all go to show that Florio deliberately meant to revive the feud.

Therefore when Eliot launched his pro-English, anti-alien dialogues in 1593 it was natural that Florio, among all the refugee modern-language teachers, should come in for the largest share of parody and satire because he alone among them had been intentionally provocative by recalling in his dialogues what his friend Bruno had said about England. It is clear that Eliot recognised the allusions to the *Cena de le ceneri* in the *Second Fruits* for into his parody of Florio's description of England he inserted a long and frenzied defence of all the colleges of Oxford and Cambridge, fiercely claiming that these are infinitely superior to any seats of learning to be found abroad. Now Florio had not said in his dialogues anything detrimental to English universities, but Eliot saw through Nolano, Torquato and Nundinio back to Bruno and was here answering, not the *Second Fruits*, but the *Cena* itself.

In this way, therefore, the memory of Bruno's Copernican dialogues was dragged into Eliot's anti-alien attack on Florio.

Raleigh, Chapman and the members of the "School of Night" were deeply interested in the new astronomy, and a large part of the satire of *Love's Labour's Lost* is aimed at their absorption in studies of this nature.

> These earthly godfathers of heaven's lights,
> That give a name to every fixéd star,
> Have no more profit of their shining nights,
> Than those that walk and wot not what they are.

There is little doubt that by the constant talk about stars and other heavenly bodies in the play and by the overthrow of the plans made by the young men for a close course of study, particularly astronomical and mathematical study, Shakespeare intended to ridicule the students of such sciences. Through his public support of Bruno, Florio must have been known as a Copernican and therefore he has a right to a part in the play's satire on the grounds of being a mathematical and astronomical "fantastic", like Raleigh, Chapman or Hariot, as well as on the grounds already described. And Eliot's dislike of Florio's revival of memories of the *Cena de le ceneri* suggests that he may have been an anti-Copernican, as indeed his antipathy to "artists" would also indicate. Here again, therefore, we seem to detect Shakespeare with Eliot and against Florio.

All this would be more convincing if it could be proved that Bruno's visit to England influenced in any way the minds of Raleigh and his friends of the "School of Night".

Had the presence of Bruno in London for two years and the publication of numbers of his works in this country during that time any influence upon the subsequent formation of Sir Walter Raleigh's school? This problem has been vaguely debated from time to time but has never been seriously and thoroughly investigated. It is a question which is worthy of greater space and attention than can here be devoted to it, but the following points may suffice to show that it ought certainly to be answered in the affirmative. In the first place there seems every probability that through his friendship with Mauvissière Raleigh came across Bruno personally and these two, once they had met, could hardly have failed to recognise one another as kindred spirits. In the second place, it can be proved that Hariot, the chief mathematical brain and exponent of Copernicus in Raleigh's group, was familiar with Bruno's works.

In a remarkable paper on Hariot which she read to the Elizabethan Literary Society in February 1933, Miss Ethel Seaton said that she had found Bruno mentioned in Hariot's papers. Every now and then in the corner of some page of calculations Hariot jots down a little list of memoranda and one such jotting contains the following:

Nolanus de immenso & mundi.[1]

This seems to be, as Miss Seaton observed, a confusion of the titles of two of Bruno's works, *De immenso*, and *De l'infinito universo et mondi*. Further, Sir William Lower in a letter to Hariot mentions Bruno and evidently assumes that his correspondent is thoroughly familiar with the arguments of the Italian philosopher. Lower was one of Hariot's pupils and admirers. From his house on the green hill-top of Trefenty, about nine miles from Carmarthen in South Wales, Lower surveyed the heavens through one of Hariot's "perspective trunks". He often corresponded with the great mathematician on matters of scientific interest. The following is an extract from a letter written by Lower to Hariot on 21 June 1610:

... just at the instante that I receaved your letters wee Traventane[2] Philosophers were a consideringe of Kepler's reasons by wch he indeauors to ouerthrow Nolanus and Gilberts opinions concerninge the immensitie of the spheare of the starres and that opinion particularlie of Nolanus by wch he affirmed that the eye beinge placed in anie parte of the vnivers the apparence would

[1] British Museum, Additional MSS. 6788, f. 67 verso.
[2] That is, philosophers of Tra'venti, or Trefenty, the name of Lower's house. One of Lower's neighbours, Sir William Protheroe, was also a pupil of Hariot and deeply interested in these studies. There was quite a little group of astronomers in South Wales at this time. (See an article by Arthur Mee on "Carmarthenshire and Early Telescopes" in *Transactions of the Carmarthenshire Antiquarian Society*, IV, 43-4.) The home of Florio's curious Welsh friend, William Vaughan, was at Torycoed in the parish of Llangendeirne which is within calling distance of Trefenty, but I have not so far been able to connect him in any way with Hariot and Lower. But Florio's other Welsh friend, Matthew Gwinne, knew Bruno very well and had a marked scientific bent. Lower himself was not a Welshman, but came into the property at Trefenty through his marriage with Penelope Perrot, daughter of Sir Thomas Perrot and Dorothy, *née* Devereux, who afterwards married the Earl of Northumberland.

be still all one as vnto us here. When I was a sayinge that although Kepler had sayd somethinge to most that mighte be vrged for that opinion of Nolanus, yet of one principall thinge hee had not thought. . . .[1]

To find Lower writing in this way concerning the "opinion of Nolanus" to Hariot, evidently assuming that the latter is familiar with that opinion, is an important witness to the truth of our contention that Bruno influenced Sir Walter Raleigh's school. Hariot was the chief mathematical brain of that school, a brain capable of grasping the implications of the Copernican theory, as Bruno had done, and of taking a long step forward from these premisses. Perhaps Hariot's most important contribution to the extension of knowledge was his study of the nature of light and the allied problem of optics, and Lower's quotation of the opinion of Nolanus concerning the eye might suggest that it was Bruno's work which gave Hariot the intellectual stimulus which was the motive power of his advance.[2]

There are points in the official examination into the "atheism" of Raleigh and his associates[3] which might be taken as indications that some of their views were not dissimilar to those of Bruno. One of the questions which the witnesses were to be asked was whether they had ever heard it said that "a mans soule shoulde dye & become like the soule of a beaste, or such like". One of the examinees said that Carew Raleigh had had some dispute with Ironside concerning the nature or substance of the soul, "and yet he remembereth he harde Mr. Carew Rawleigh saye at Gillingham there was a god in nature".

---

[1] Quoted by Henry Stevens, *Thomas Hariot and his Associates,* 1900, p. 117. The reference for the original is British Museum, Additional MSS. 6789, ff. 425–6.

[2] Hariot was not in England at the time of Bruno's visit, so he must have acquired his knowledge of the Italian philosopher's thought by reading or conversation with others.

[3] The papers relating to this enquiry are printed in Dr G. B. Harrison's edition of *Willobie His Avisa,* 1926, pp. 255–71.

This question and answer have a Pythagorean and pantheistic air strongly reminiscent of Bruno's ideas. Again, in the dispute at Sir George Trenchard's table, Sir Walter Raleigh leads Ironside to entangle himself in his Aristotelian definitions rather in the manner in which Bruno tripped up Torquato and Nundinio at the Ash Wednesday supperparty. Francis Osborne said that "Sir Walter Ralegh was the first that ventured to tack about, and sailed aloof from the beaten track of the Schools; therefore...he was ever after branded with the title of an atheist, though a known asserter of God and Providence".[1] This could also be said of Bruno.

The members of Raleigh's circle shared Bruno's admiration for Pythagoras. The Earl of Northumberland, who was one of the most enthusiastic devotees of the new studies inaugurated by Raleigh and Hariot, was addressed by George Peele in 1593, or thereabouts, in the following terms:

> ...Renownèd lord, Northumberland's fair flower,
> The Muses' love, patron, and favourite,
> That artisans and scholars dost embrace,
> And clothest Mathesis in rich ornaments;
> That admirable mathematic skill,
> Familiar with the stars and zodiac,
> To whom the heaven lies open as her book;
> By whose directions undeceivable,
> Leaving our schoolmen's vulgar trodden paths,
> And following the ancient reverend steps
> Of Trismegistus and Pythagoras,
> Through uncouth ways and unaccessible,
> Dost pass into the spacious pleasant fields
> Of divine science and philosophy;
> From whence beholding the deformities
> Of common errors, and world's vanity,

---

[1] In his preface to *Miscellany of Sundry Essayes, Paradoxes and Problematical discourses, letters and characters*, 1659. See J. Beau, "La Religion de Sir Walter Ralegh", *Revue Anglo-Américaine*, June 1934.

Dost here enjoy that sacred sweet content
That baser souls, not knowing, not affect:
And so by Fate's and Fortune's good aspéct
Raised, in thy height, and these unhappy times,
Disfurnish'd wholly of heroical spirits
That learning should with glorious hands uphold,
(For who should learning underbear but he
That knows thereof the precious worthiness,
And seeks true science from base vanity?)
Hast in regard the true philosophy
That in pure wisdom seats her happiness.[1]

To anyone familiar with Bruno's outlook these lines will not sound strange. The reverence for mathematics, and for Pythagoras, the contempt for the trodden paths of the schoolmen, the proud sense of superior knowledge and illumination hidden from baser souls, the praise of "heroical spirits"[2] for whom true learning and philosophy constitute the highest happiness—such matters were the constant theme of Bruno's conversation and writings. Those who would seek for Bruno's influence in England should, in my opinion, study the output of the Raleigh group, on its poetic no less than on its scientific side. For if Hariot was mainly interested in Bruno's opinion concerning the eye, who shall say how much the heroic fury of Marlowe's high-aspiring mind, the neo-Platonic yearnings of Raleigh, the nocturnal obscurities of Chapman, owe to the great Italian? These suggestions also affect the study of Spenser, whose debt to Bruno has so often been discussed; for if Bruno's ideas were familiar to the Raleigh circle, the probability that they were also familiar to Spenser becomes much greater.

It is sometimes forgotten that the men of the Renaissance went back to classical origins, and particularly to Greek

---

[1] George Peele, *The Honour of the Garter.* See Peele, *Works,* ed. A. H. Bullen, 1888, II, 316-20.

[2] One of Bruno's works is called *De gli eroici furori.*

origins, for inspiration in the development of the scientific side of their thought, as well as the purely humanistic or literary. There was a special affinity between the modern "Copernicans" and the ancient "Pythagoreans". The Pythagorean astronomy differed from the other conceptions of antiquity in attributing a planetary motion to the earth and was thus nearer in spirit to the new ideas than any other system. When the Church condemned the Copernican theory, its heathen and "Pythagorean" character was one of the charges against it. Pythagoreans had an almost mystical reverence for "number" as being in itself the essence of reality; and Pythagoras was Bruno's favourite philosopher. According to Peele, he was also the guide of the Earl of Northumberland and, therefore, doubtless, of other members of the "School of Night".

This fact, that Copernicans were associated with the philosophy of Pythagoras, might be of assistance in the detection of satire on the "School of Night" in *Love's Labour's Lost*. And here I think that Warburton should be given a little credit for having made the following observation in 1747. He thought that Berowne's use of the word "numbers" was interesting.

> For when would you, my liege, or you, or you,
> In leaden contemplation have found out
> Such fiery *numbers* as the prompting eyes
> Of beauty's tutors have enriched you with?[1]

In connection with this Warburton observes:

Alluding to the discoveries in modern astronomy; at that time greatly improving, in which the ladies eyes are compared, as usual to *stars*. He calls them *numbers*, alluding to the *Pythagorean* principles of astronomy, which were founded on the laws of harmony.[2]

[1] IV. iii. 317–20.
[2] *The Works of Shakespear...collated..corrected and emended...by Mr. Pope and Mr. Warburton*, 1747, II, 246.

When we remember that Copernicans in those days were also Pythagoreans, Warburton's gloss illuminates these lines as containing a pun on "numbers" in the sense of the poems which the lords have just written to the ladies and "number" in the Pythagorean sense in which the members of the "School of Night" reverenced it. Berowne thus twice contradicts Chapman by preferring love and ladies' eyes to "night" and "numbers". If Berowne's "numbers" were Pythagorean numbers his subsequent exquisite and famous lines,

> For valour, is not Love a Hercules,
> Still climbing trees in the Hesperides?
> Subtle as Sphinx, as sweet and musical
> As bright Apollo's lute, strung with his hair;
> And, when Love speaks, the voice of all the gods
> Make heaven drowsy with the harmony,[1]

probably contain some memory of the mathematical intervals in music and of the harmony of the spheres, both of which conceptions were associated with Pythagoras.

There are other uses of "number" in the play which might have had a similar application. Rosaline asks Berowne how many steps are "numbered" in the miles which he and his friends have travelled to visit her. Berowne replies,

> We number nothing that we spend for you.[2]

Just before this the king, Rosaline, and Boyet use the verb "measure" seven times in eight lines when discussing how many steps and inches there are in the miles the men have traversed. All this points, I think, at astronomical measurements and Pythagorean "number" and the allusion is brought in at the moment when the gallants show by coming to visit the princess and her ladies that they have abandoned such studies.

[1] IV. iii. 337–42.
[2] V. ii. 198. See also V. ii. 35 where Rosaline discusses Berowne's verses. "The numbers true, and were the numb'ring too."

Pythagoreans dwelt much upon the opposition of odd and even in numbers. "The odd number was identified with the limited, the even with the unlimited, because even numbers may be perpetually halved, whereas the odd numbers (at least the earlier ones), being without factors, seem to stand in solid singleness."[1] The number four was held by Pythagoras and his followers to be particularly sacred because it is the first square number.

> The Fox, the Ape, and the Humble-bee,
> Were still *at odds*, being but *three*.
> Until the Goose came out of door,
> Staying *the odds* by adding *four*.[2]

There is probably a memory of some jargon familiar to the "School of Night" in this and other passages hinting at "number". When it is discovered that Berowne, as well as the other three men, is in love, Dumaine says:

Dumaine. Now the *number* is *even.*
Berowne.   True true, we are *four*.[3]

Not only did the new science grow out of Greek science, but there was also Greek precedent for mocking at scientists, and all their "measuring" and "numbering", in a satirical comedy. In his *Birds*, Aristophanes laughs at the sudden passion for science amongst the Athenians of his day. An astronomer called Meton is introduced, who is encumbered

---

[1] *Encyclopædia Britannica*, article on Pythagoras. Of course Bruno was not the only Italian Copernican of the period who admired Pythagoras. Signor Benedetto Croce has in his *Nuove curiosità storiche* (1922) an interesting chapter on Italian books on the mystery of number. Decio Celere in his *Sommaria descrittione dell' Heroe*, 1607, describes the *four* grades through which "l' uomo studioso" must pass before arriving "alla grandezza heroica". There is in existence a manuscript discourse, by a certain Luca Auriemma, on "Three", in which substances are arranged in trilogies and a series of proverbs in three clauses are collected.

[2] III. i. 94-7.   [3] IV. iii. 207.

with a quantity of instruments with which he proposes to take measurements. He is told to

> Get out, you coxcomb, find out by your Geometry,
> The road you came, and measure it back: you'd best.[1]

This is the same kind of joke as that made by Shakespeare in *Love's Labour's Lost* who makes his would-be learned gentlemen measure many miles to tread a measure with the ladies on the grass.

Nothing definite could be deduced from the somewhat similar attitude to scientists adopted by Shakespeare and Aristophanes. A comparison of *The Birds* with *Love's Labour's Lost*, and it is a comparison which it is worth while to make with some care, would merely suggest that these two great comic geniuses thought independently along the same lines when confronted by similar situations. *But*, let us remember that Eliot suggested that a comedy like those of Aristophanes might be made out of the pretensions of the aliens. *And*, Eliot actually mentions *The Birds* in his last dialogue.

> Without doubt men haue learned Musicke of Birdes.
> Democritus vvas the Nightingales scholler, witnesse
> Aristophanes in his comedie of the song of Birdes.[2]

Does not *Love's Labour's Lost* end with the songs of two birds, the owl and the cuckoo? And did not Florio lament that Aristophanes and his comedians had made plays and scoured their mouths on Socrates? It begins almost to look as though the idea of making a comedy out of all these "artists", for which there was precedent in Aristophanes, might have occurred to Shakespeare one day when conversing with his "villanist" friend Eliot. Eliot's conversa-

---

[1] *The Birds*, ll. 1019–20. (*The Plays of Aristophanes*, translated by J. H. Frere (Everyman's Library), I, 182.)

[2] *Ortho-epia Gallica*, sig. *v*1; *Parlement of Pratlers*, p. 106.

tion seems to have been stimulating. We know that it suggested a title to Harvey.

*   *   *   *

The fact that the memory of Bruno's Copernican dialogues comes into Eliot's attack on Florio and the other refugee aliens gives us a connection between the "star" jokes and the "schoolmaster" jokes in the play. We see that Florio's identification with Bruno's point of view associated him in some degree with the "School of Night". And once again we seem to detect Eliot and Shakespeare in agreement.

CHAPTER VI

Bruno and "Stella"

Bruno is one of the people whose presence has been suspected in *Love's Labour's Lost* though that theory has very few, if any, supporters to-day in England. Apologists for it have pointed out that "Berowne" is made at one point to rhyme with "moon", indicating that the name was pronounced "Beroon". The vowel and consonant sounds of "Beroon" and "Bruno" have much in common. The word "bruno" means "dark" in Italian; "dark" is a word which is constantly bandied about in the play. The influence of Bruno has been, however, more commonly sought in *Hamlet* than in *Love's Labour's Lost*. At one time much study was devoted to the problem of whether or not Hamlet betrays any knowledge of Bruno's philosophy. The question was debated at the end of the last century, mostly by German scholars, and it was finally answered in the negative.[1] The point was made that nowhere in all his works does Shakespeare show any clear knowledge of the Copernican system. To the end of his life the great dramatist appears to have been content to walk a fixed earth. Whenever he has occasion to speak of natural phenomena connected with the universal frame he uses the terms of the old Ptolemaic system:

> As when the golden sun salutes the morn,
> And, having gilt the ocean with his beams,
> Gallops the zodiac in his glistering coach,
> And overlooks the highest-peering hills....[2]

[1] By R. Beyersdorff, "Giordano Bruno und Shakespeare", in *Jahrbuch der Deutschen Shakespeare-Gesellschaft*, XXVI, 1891, 259–324. For the positive view see W. König, "Shakespeare und Giordano Bruno", *Ibid.*, XI, 1876, 97–139. A more recent essay by P. Orano, *Amleto è Giordano Bruno?* 1916, is not of much value.

[2] *Titus Andronicus*, II. i. 5–8.

Therefore, say the opponents of the Bruno theory, since Shakespeare appears to know nothing of the discoveries of Copernicus, he cannot have known much about Bruno. And although much energy has been spent in trying to find traces of Bruno's pantheism in Hamlet's philosophy and in the sonnets, it is impossible to prove any such connection. The conclusion was therefore reached, and is to-day almost universally held, that it is entirely fanciful to see Bruno in any of Shakespeare's plays.

The arguments are perfectly sound but the conclusion is, in my opinion, too hastily reached. Certainly there is little trace in Shakespeare of the Copernican astronomy and no definite trace of Bruno's characteristic pantheism. But the conclusion to reach from that premiss is that Shakespeare either had not read Bruno's works or did not approve of them, from which it does not necessarily follow that he had not heard of Bruno.

Although not himself a Copernican, he knew that some people in his day and generation, some "earthly godfathers of heaven's lights" were busily engaged in astronomical studies. If Shakespeare can allude to the "School of Night" without being a Copernican himself, why should he not also allude to Bruno with whom we have seen that Raleigh's coterie had some connection? There is no reason at all why superficial rumours of the Italian philosopher and his ideas should not have reached Shakespeare, for, as we saw in the last chapter, Florio's and Eliot's dialogues are a channel of communication which lead right back to Bruno.

I am not the first to view the Bruno problem in this light. In 1922 Signor Croce quoted a friend of his as having suggested that since Florio introduced Bruno into the *Second Fruits* as "Nolano", Shakespeare might have introduced him into *Love's Labour's Lost*.[1] In repeating

[1] Benedetto Croce, *Nuove Curiosità Storiche*, 1922, pp. 121-2. See also V. Spampanato, *Vita di Giordano Bruno*, 1921, I, 357 ff.

this suggestion Signor Croce emphasises the point which
I have just emphasised, namely that such a hypothesis
would not involve one in any assumptions as to the influence
of the Brunian philosophy upon Shakespeare but would be
restricted to "la probabile aneddotica della vita londinese,
nella quale la figura di Bruno non passò inosservata".

We have seen that one "anecdote of Bruno's London
life", namely his quarrels with the English Aristotelians
and his strictures on Oxford, was reflected from Florio to
Eliot and so played a part in that situation between Eliot
and the foreign pedagogues which is certainly one of the
ingredients of Shakespeare's comedy. Was there any other
"anecdote" about him of which Florio and Eliot show
knowledge? The answer to that question is that there was,
and that the elucidation of this second Bruno rumour will
partially explain the connection between the "stars" in
Love's Labour's Lost—the astronomical observations of
the "School of Night"—and the "ladies' eyes" with
which they are so constantly contrasted.

*   *   *   *

It is well known that endless arguments on the subject
of love and of women were a notable feature of the Italian
Renaissance. Academies, or courts of love, flourished, in
which polite persons of both sexes met for the Platonic
discussion of love problems. The Petrarchist bowed down
before Woman and worshipped her as his goddess, holy
and remote, cruel but exquisite, in whose beauty heaven
was revealed. The anti-Petrarchist scoffed at these chival-
rous exaggerations and hesitations. Woman was no goddess
but a being much inferior to man, created for the gratifica-
tion of man's senses and for the continuation of the race
but otherwise of very little use. Far from being icily
remote and of miraculous beauty, she was always unchaste
and unfaithful, often ugly, and generally stupid and a

shrew. It was a kind of fashionable literary game to state these two irreconcilable views side by side, leaving it to the reader to make his choice between them. Bruno often introduced matter of this kind into his philosophical dialogues.

The Englishman with whom Bruno had most to do during his two years' stay in London, and whom he mentions most frequently in his works was Sir Philip Sidney. Two of his philosophical dialogues were dedicated to Sidney, and one of these dedications—that to *De gli eroici furori* (1585) opens with a violent attack on woman-worship.

To fix all one's thought and study upon the beauty of a woman's body is, O most generous knight, the mark of a base, brutish, and filthy mind. Good God! what more vile, what more ignoble spectacle can present itself to a wholesome eye than that of a man who is dreamy, afflicted, tormented, sad, melancholy, now hot, now cold, now fervent, now fearful, now pale, now red, with countenance now perplexed, now resolute, who spends the best part of his time, the best part of his fleeting life distilling the elixir of his brain in writing down and publicly recording the perpetual tortures, the heavy torments, the weary thoughts and speeches, the bitter meditations generated beneath the tyranny of an unworthy, imbecile, infatuated, wanton, filthy wretch of a woman?[1]

This is the purest anti-Petrarchism. The writings in which the elixir of the brain is distilled and love-torments are publicly recorded are the sonnets which the Petrarchist writes to a mistress. Such activity is a stupid waste of time, says Bruno, and women are not worth it. By all means let a man enjoy women, he goes on to say, treating them as they should be treated, namely as women and not as goddesses, but let him not waste the energies of his mind upon them, those intellectual forces which should be

---

[1] G. Bruno, *Opere italiane*, ed. G. Gentile, second edition, 1927, II, 309. Quoted as translated in *John Florio*, pp. 104–5.

devoted to the search for truth and the contemplation of the divine.

The surprising feature of this tirade is the fact that it was addressed to Sidney—to "Astrophel", the humble worshipper of "Stella", who had distilled his brain into those famous sonnets which, though not to be printed for some years yet, were passed from hand to hand in manuscript and formed the wonder and admiration of his friends. It would seem that Bruno was not blundering in ignorance here but that he was perfectly well aware of the "Stella" affair, for towards the end of the dedication he makes a cautious reservation to his anti-Petrarchist attack on the idealisation of women. Remembering the trouble which his complaints about England in the *Cena* had brought upon him he exempts the women of England, and above all that Divine Lady who reigns over England, from his strictures. The women of England, and particularly those who are connected with Sidney by personal ties, "must not be esteemed a part of the feminine sex for they are not women but nymphs, but goddesses, and of celestial substance". He is a Petrarchist when he speaks of Sidney's English goddesses but an anti-Petrarchist to the rest of the female human race. The dedication concludes with an adulatory sonnet to the ladies of England and to that "unique Diana" who reigns over them. She is their sun, and they are not women, but nymphs, goddesses, *stars*,

E siete in terra quel ch'in ciel *le stelle*.[1]

We have Florio's authority for believing that Bruno meant this as an allusion to the lady to whom Sidney addressed his sonnets under the pseudonym of "Stella".

Who was the "Stella" whom Sidney loved? The traditional view is that she was Penelope Rich, *née* Devereux,

[1] *Opere italiane, ed. cit.* II, 330.

the sister of the Earl of Essex; but as some doubt has recently been thrown upon this identification (upon which some of our future arguments depend) it will be as well to take a glance at the evidence for it.[1]

One of the three dedications in the 1603 edition of Florio's *Montaigne* is addressed to the Countess of Rutland and Lady Penelope Rich. It is followed by a sonnet to Lady Rich by Matthew Gwinne who signs it with his pseudonym of "Il Candido".[2] This sonnet runs as follows:

To the Honorably-vertuous Ladie,
La: Penelope Riche.

Madame, to write of you, and doe you right,
  What meane we, or what meanes to ayde meane might?
  Since HE, who admirably did endite,
  Entiteling you Perfections heire, Ioyes light,
Loves life, Lifes gemme, Vertues court, Heav'ns delight,
  Natures chiefe worke, Fair'st booke, his Muses spright,
  Heav'n on Earth, peerelesse Phœnix, *Phœbe* bright,
  Yet said, he was to seeke, of you to write.
Vnlesse your selfe be of your selfe devising;
  Or that another such you can inspire.
  Inspire you can; but ô none such can be:
Your selfe as bright as your mid-day, as rising.
  Yet, though we but repeate who would flie higher,
  And though we but translate, take both in gree.

Il Candido.[3]

---

[1] Since writing this chapter I find that the evidence for Lady Rich as "Stella" has been ably set forth by Hoyt H. Hudson, "Penelope Devereux as Sidney's Stella", in the *Huntington Library Bulletin*, No. 7, April 1935, pp. 89–129. Mr Hudson not only works out more fully than I have done here the implications of Gwinne's sonnet but he brings together a mass of other evidence which establishes beyond any possibility of doubt that the traditional identification of "Stella" with Lady Rich is quite correct.

[2] It is commonly stated in error that this sonnet is by Florio.

[3] The dedication and the sonnets are printed in Florio's *Montaigne*, ed. J. I. M. Stewart, Nonesuch Press, 1931, II, 564–68.

Gwinne has here strung together a list of epithets which
Sidney had applied to "Stella":

> And, not content to be Perfection's heire.[1]
>   . . . but now appeares my day
> The onely light of joy,[2]
> But that rich foole, who by blind Fortune's lot
> The richest gemme of love and life enjoyes..[3]
> Queene Vertue's Court, which some call Stella's face..[4]
> When Nature made her chiefe worke, Stella's eyes..[5]
> Who will in fairest booke of Nature know..[6]
> When I demaund of Phœnix Stella's state..[7]

It is thus abundantly clear that when Gwinne tells Lady
Rich of the "HE" who wrote of her in these ways he means
that she was Sidney's "Stella".

Florio's dedication, which precedes this sonnet, includes
the Countess of Rutland, who was Sidney's daughter, as
well as Lady Rich. Speaking to these two ladies of Sidney's
Arcadia Florio says,

I know, nor this, nor any I have seen, or can conceive, in this
or other language, can in aught be compared to that perfect-
vnperfect *Arcadia*, which all our world yet weepes with you, that
your all praise-exceeding father (his praise-succeeding Countess)
your worthy friend (friend-worthiest Lady) lived not to mend or
end-it.[8]

"Your worthy friend", says Florio to Lady Rich, speaking
of Sidney. Evidently he, as well as Gwinne, believed that
she was "Stella".

Florio and Gwinne had every reason to know what they
were talking about. Although it was not until 1603 that
they wrote thus, they could both go back in memory to

---

[1] *Astrophel and Stella*, Sonnet LXXI, l. 9.
[2] Sonnet LXXVI, ll. 3–4.   [3] Sonnet XXIV, ll. 9–10.
[4] Sonnet IX, l. 1.   [5] Sonnet VII, l. 1.
[6] Sonnet LXXI, l. 1.   [7] Sonnet XCII, l. 6.
[8] See *John Florio*, pp. 199–200.

the days when Sidney was alive and when Bruno was in
London. They both knew Lady Rich personally. Their
evidence as to her identity with "Stella" is clear and out-
spoken and, when taken in conjunction with the internal
evidence in the sonnets themselves, notably the very obvious
play on the word "rich", it renders any efforts to prove
the contrary quite superfluous.

Florio also makes it clear that when Bruno apostrophised
the ladies of England as "stars" in the sonnet prefixed
to his *Eroici Furori*,

E siete in terra quel ch'in ciel le stelle,

he was thinking of Lady Rich as "Stella". Addressing
both the Countess of Rutland and Lady Rich, Florio says,

...as my fellow *Nolano* in his heroycall furies wrote (noble
Countesse) to your most heroicke father, & in a sonnet to you
Ladies of *England, You are not women, but their likenesse Nymphs,
Goddesses, and of Celestiall substance.*

Et siete in terra quel' ch'in ciel' le stelle,
And above all, that onely divine Diana,
Qual' è tra voi quel che tra gl' astri il sole.

Since he carefully reminds Lady Rich of the "stars" line
he evidently thought that Bruno meant that line as an
allusion to "Stella". We thus have Florio's evidence to
support the view that when Bruno addressed his anti-
Petrarchist tirade to Sidney, he knew of the latter's
romance with Lady Rich and that he was engaged in
"writing down and publicly recording" his feelings for
her—a kind of activity which the Nolan so rudely con-
demns in the opening paragraph of his dedication.

The dialogues of the *Eroici Furori*, to which this dedication is the introduction, set forth the theme of the soul's
aspiration towards truth and knowledge through love, not
of individual women, but of the ideal, the universal, the
One. This neo-Platonic theme of heroic aspiration towards
an ideal and mystical love is expressed in sonnets in the

Petrarcan form which are interspersed in the dialogues, and which, though often using language of a Petrarcan character about blind Cupid, and other set mythological metaphors, are applied not to "some Doris, Cynthia, or Laura" but to that highest intellectual and speculative love through which Reality is discerned.

> Love, through whom high truth I do discern,
> Thou openest the black diamond doors;
> Through the eyes enters my deity, and through seeing
> Is born, lives, is nourished, and has eternal reign;
> Shows forth what heaven holds, earth and hell:
> Makes present true images of the absent;
> Gains strength: and drawing with straight aim,
> Wounds, lays bare and frets the inmost heart.
> Attend now, thou base hind unto the truth,
> Bend down the ear to my unerring word;
> Open, open, if thou canst the eyes, foolish perverted one!
> Thou understanding little, call'st him child,
> Because thou swiftly changest, fugitive he seems,
> Thyself not seeing, call'st him blind.[1]

The theme of "eyes, blindness, sight, looking, light, darkness", recurs constantly in these sonnets.

There is a kind of contradiction inherent in Bruno's thought in the *Eroici Furori*. On the one hand he seems to suggest that the spiritual love cannot be achieved without the abandonment of, or contempt for, the worldly love. But on the other hand he expounds his pantheistic philosophy which sees the spiritual and the material as fundamentally inseparable, and, viewed in this light, fleshly, sensual, or material love is not in itself evil although the lowest grade in the three stages by which the soul ascends to the knowledge of divine or intellectual love. Bruno despises the timid inhibitions of the Petrarchist's approach to his mistress,

---

[1] L. Williams, *The Heroic Enthusiasts*, 1887, Part I, p. 50. This is the only English translation of the *Eroici Furori*, and it omits the dedication to Sidney. Also it is now out of print and unobtainable.

which were the outcome of the mediaeval ascetic ideal, but he does not make his own attitude very clear. As Professor Elton puts it, "Love to him is now a gaily Lampsacene appetite, now a purely intellectual rage, and is identical with the philosophic thirst for immersion in the supreme unity."[1]

It is to me most surprising that the dedication and contents of the *Eroici Furori*—a work which was publicly offered to Sidney by Bruno—have not been more closely studied in connection with Sidney's sonnets. Whether or not any of the latter were composed late enough to have been actually influenced by Bruno, it seems to me obvious that the Italian must have been taken to a considerable extent into Sidney's confidence. How constantly throughout the *Astrophel and Stella* sequence does its author ask himself whether writing sonnets to Stella is an occupation worthy of one who feels at heart that he ought to be bending the forces of his nature towards higher things?

> Reason, in faith thou art well serv'd, that still
> Wouldst brabling be with sence and Love in me;
> I rather wisht thee clime the Muses' hill;
> Or reach the fruite of Nature's choisest tree;
> Or seeke heav'n's course or heavn'n's inside to see.[2]

The same gnawing doubt is expressed in the famous,

> With what sharpe checkes I in my selfe am shent
> When into Reason's audite I do go,[3]

and Reason tells him that his "youth doth waste", his "knowledge brings forth toyes". He reads Plato (the guiding spirit of the *Eroici Furori*) and such reading warns him

> that to my birth I owe
> Nobler desires, least else that friendly foe,
> Great expectation, weare a traine of shame.[4]

---

[1] O. Elton, *Modern Studies*, 1907, p. 29.   [2] Sonnet x, ll. 1–5.
[3] Sonnet xviii, ll. 1–2.   [4] Sonnet xxi, ll. 6–8.

"Come let me write!" he cries, and then is seized with the query,

> But will not wise men thinke thy words fond ware?[1]

And then there is the great sonnet in which he finally breaks away from his obsession.

> Leave me, O Love, which reachest but to dust;
> And thou, my mind, aspire to higher things;
> Grow rich in that which never taketh rust;
> What ever fades, but fading pleasure brings.
> Draw in thy beames, and humble all thy might
> To that sweet yoke where lasting freedomes be;
> Which breakes the clowdes, and opens forth the light,
> That doth both shine, and give us sight to see.
> O take fast hold; let that light be thy guide
> In this small course which birth drawes out to death,
> And think how evill becommeth him to slide,
> Who seeketh heav'n, and comes of heav'nly breath.
> Then farewell, world; thy uttermost I see:
> Eternall Love, maintaine thy life in me.

The pious Petrarchist might sometimes wearily turn to God away from his love-torments, but in general he regarded the beauty of his mistress as a "ladder to the maker", an idea of which there is little trace in Sidney. This dualism in Sidney's mind is generally ascribed to his Puritan leanings and to the influence of his friend Hubert Languet, but the vague, Platonic nature of his aspirations towards the divine, his feeling that it is towards the pursuit of knowledge, even of science or astronomy (he wants to reach the fruit of Nature's choicest tree, to seek heaven's course, and heaven's inside to see) that his energies would be better directed are not really in the accepted Puritan vein.

Such an attitude is, however, reflected in Bruno's *Eroici Furori* with its anti-Petrarchistic preface and the Platonic idealism of its dialogues. Bruno was very far from being a Puritan, but in spite of his belief that matter and spirit are

---

[1] Sonnet XXXIV, l. 7.

one, that God *is* nature, he could not shake off an instinctive dualism, an instinctive contempt for the miserable world of appearances. As De Sanctis acutely remarks, what we are really confronted with here is probably the difference between the philosopher and the poet. A man like Bruno "was intended from the beginning to speculate on the One, the Same, and the Identical, but not to make works of art. He never goes down into his world, but is always outside of it, seeing it in its generalities".[1] But poetry is the exact opposite of this. "Poetry is the giving of value to even the smallest phenomena of life."[2]

Personally I think that some of Sidney's sonnets may be late enough to have been written under Bruno's influence. Why, one may ask, do Bruno's associates, Florio and Gwinne, give themselves such knowing airs about Lady Rich and "Stella"? But whether or not this is conceded, it is I think self-evident, that the *Eroici Furori*, written by a man who knew Sidney personally and knew of his "Stella" romance, constitutes a guide to Sidney's state of mind which cannot be neglected. And the evidence of the *Eroici Furori* suggests that *Astrophel and Stella* may reflect, not so much the struggles of a Puritan with the flesh, as the struggles of a philosopher with distractions. Astrophel the poet is always being bullied by Astrophel the philosopher and sternly told that it is a waste of time to observe the unfashionable and yet fascinating blackness of Stella's eyes when knowledge in its pure essence, to seek heaven's course and heaven's inside to see, is the only goal worth striving after.

Bruno's *Eroici Furori* dedication must have been something of a sensation in cultured circles at the time. For although he so pointedly set the lunar queen of England and her stellar ladies above all criticism, it is impossible to disguise the fact that the Nolan addressed to Sidney—to

[1] Francesco de Sanctis, *History of Italian Literature*, translated by Joan Redfern, 1932, II, 719.   [2] *Ibid., loc. cit.*

"Astrophel" himself—a tirade against sonnet-writing and woman-worship. It was a bold, a somewhat tactless thing to do, and it may have caused irritation, as the criticism of England in the *Cena* had done. Sir Philip Sidney was already something of a national institution.

Now these memories connected with Bruno, with Sidney, with "Stella", were revived by Florio in the *Second Fruits* some years after Bruno had left England. With his usual readiness to seize upon the personal aspect of any matter, in recalling the *Cena* Florio had dwelt, as we have already seen, not upon the new Copernican astronomy therein discussed, but upon Bruno's quarrels with the English doctors and the anti-alien feelings which these had aroused. In the same way when the Italian teacher alludes to the *Eroici Furori* in his *Second Fruits*, as he does, it is not in order to discuss the relation of matter to spirit, or high philosophical themes of that kind, but to remind his readers of Bruno, of Sidney and "Stella", and of the fascinating Petrarcan and anti-Petrarcan arguments.

The last chapter of the *Second Fruits* consists of pleasant and proverbial discourse on the subject of love and of women. This is the longest of all the dialogues—it occupies about a quarter of the whole book—and it abounds with memories of Bruno. A passage in Bruno's *De la Causa* in which a grammatical argument was used in favour of women, and the vices were said to be masculine nouns while the virtues are feminine, is quoted at length by Florio.[1] Besides actually quoting from Bruno's writings Florio recalls his whole ambiguous treatment of the "woman" question, by setting out the Petrarcan and the anti-Petrarcan arguments side by side. In Florio's dialogue "Siluestro" supports the Petrarcan side, whilst "Pandolpho" is a virulent anti-Petrarchist. Siluestro calls women "goddesses" and worships them idolatrously; he

[1] The parallel passages from the *Causa* and *Second Fruits* are quoted in full by V. Spampanato, *La Critica*, XXII, 123, 246–7.

uses much mythical material about Cupid, Diana, and so on, and quotes extensively from Petrarch. For Pandolpho, women are worthless, contemptible creatures. He draws his anti-female material mainly from proverbs of which he has an astonishing supply at his fingers' ends. That Florio deliberately meant all this to remind the reader of the problems raised in the *Eroici Furori* is indicated by the fact that he mentions Sidney, and how Sidney traced the descent of Cupid from Argus of the hundred eyes (an allusion to a poem in the *Arcadia*), following this up with a recollection of Plato, and how Plato distinguished between a "beastly, vulgare, and voluptuous loue" and a "celestiall loue, the auctor, maister, and preseruer of all things".[1] I believe that Florio was thinking, and meant his readers to think, of how Bruno had displayed to Sidney the contrast between a trivial earthly love and the heroic fury with which Platonic or intellectual love should be pursued.

Florio places his love-dialogue in a setting of night and star-light. The words with which it opens are,

This wilbe a faire moone and starre-shine night, my companions, and fine to watch in.[2]

The night and the stars recall Bruno's astronomical speculations but they also recall the "Stella" theme. At the end of the dialogue Florio sets Queen Elizabeth, "the woman of women of this age", and the ladies of her court altogether above and outside of the whole argument, comparing them to the moon and the stars.

...as we reioyce now to beholde the heauen bespangled with so many twinckling starres, and eyed lights (all which are women) with their threefould queene, that is to say Luna in heauen, Cinthia or Diana on earth, & Proserpina in hell, euen so the heauens & all they reioyce to looke downward, and with so many eyes behold so many fayre & good women which now liue to the honour & seruice of the woman of women of this age.... [3]

[1] The passage is quoted in *John Florio*, pp. 121-2.
[2] *Second Fruits*, sig. Y 3.   [3] *Ibid.* sigs. Dd 2, Dd 3.

Since Florio in 1603 reminded Lady Rich of Bruno's sonnet in which Elizabeth was called "l'unica Diana" and the women of England "stelle", it is legitimate to conclude that in this passage in the *Second Fruits*, published in 1591, he was also recalling Bruno's poem with its implication that one of the "stars" was "Stella".

A contemporary learning Italian from the *Second Fruits* and possessing friends who were well versed in court and literary gossip would understand all this. Moreover, to such a contemporary this star-spangled love-dialogue would seem the most fascinating feature of Florio's manual. Remember that 1591, the year in which the *Second Fruits* was published, was the moment when many of the Elizabethan sonneteers were busily writing the sonnets which they were afterwards to publish. It was in this year that the unauthorised *Astrophel and Stella*, with its preface by Nashe, was first printed, and gave a fillip to the whole movement. Florio chose the crucial moment for the launching of his love-dialogue, the Petrarcan side of which was a kind of provision of material for the use of the sonneteers. That he did this quite deliberately is indicated in the dedication of the *Second Fruits* where he says that he regards his book as "not vnfit for those that embrace the language of the muses or would beautifie their speech with a not vulgar brauery".[1]

When Eliot replied to Florio with his *Ortho-epia Gallica* he seems to have understood Florio's allusions to Bruno's quarrels with the English doctors related in the *Cena*, and to have answered these allusions by his defence of English universities. Did he also understand the allusions to the *Eroici Furori*? In order to answer this question the following rather long passage from the last dialogue of the *Ortho-epia Gallica* must be quoted and studied.

---

[1] *Second Fruits*, sig. A 4.

The "pratlers" are discussing lovers, and in particular a certain "Ieronimo Pierruche", who is in love.

This Ieronimo you knew him well fat slaue, cherrie cheeked, faire and vvell liking, merry, with a slicke face, pleasant, disposed, and a tratling companion: Now he is leane, vvan, pale, looking like one halfe dead, vveake, vgly, dreaming, louing to be alone, and cares for no bodies company: so that none of those that had seene him before, could now knowe him againe.

O the poore and wretched yoong man! Of what proceeds his griefe?

Of loue.

Of loue? Tell troth.

Now he is mad: he is foolish: oftentimes he vvalketh alone: but vvill neuer speake to any bodie: alwaies mumbling or recording some thing in English verse, that he hath made to his sweete-heart and minion.

O caitiffe boye!

One vvhile you shall see him faine a sea of teares, a lake of miseries, vvring his hands and vveep, accuse the heauen, curse the earth, make an anatomie of his heart, to freeze, to burne, to adore, to plaie the Idolater, to admire, to faine heauens, to forge hels, to counterfait Sisyphus, to play the Tantalus, to represent Titius Tragedie. And by and by he exalteth in his verses that Diana whom he loueth best: her haire is nothing but gold wire, her browes arches and vautes of Ebenus: her eies twinckling starres like Castor and Pollux, her lookes lightnings: her mouth Corall: her necke Orient-Pearle: her breath Baulme, Amber, and Muske: her throate of snow: her necke milke-white: her dugs that she hath on her brest, Mountaines or Apples of Alablaster. All the rest of her body is but a prodigalitie & treasure of heauen & of nature, that she had reserued to work the perfection of his mistres & dear.

Tis great danger least he fall beside himselfe in the end.

O the poore passionate is cruelly eclipsed! One while you shall see him drownd in teares and lamentations, to make the aire eccho with his sighs, complaints, murmurings, rages, imprecations: otherwhiles if he haue got but a glaunce of his goddesse, you shall see him gay, glistering like an Emerawd, and pleasant, sometime you shall see him crosse, passe and repasse fiue or six times a day through a street that he may haue but one friendly looke of her eye that he loueth best.

What will you giue me if I shew you a letter that he wrot to his sweet-hart.

I pray thee my minion do me this fauour that I may see it.

I will read it out aloud, hearken.

Mistresse your beautie is so excellent, so singular, so celestiall, that I beleeue Nature hath bestowed it on you as a sampler to shew how much she can do when will imploy her full power and best skill. All that is in your selfe is but honie, is but sugar, is but heauenly ambrosia. It vvas to you to whom Paris should haue iudged the golden apple, not to Venus, no, nor to Iuno, nor to Minerua, for neuer was there so great magnificence in Iuno, so great wisdome in Minerua, so great beautie in Venus, as in you. O heauens, gods and goddesses, happie shall he be to whom you grant the fauour to col you, to kisse you, and to lie with you. I cannot tell whether I am predestinated by the Fairies, wherefore I commend me to your good grace, and kissing your white hands, humbly I take my leaue without Adieu.

He vnderstands alreadie the courtisane Rhetoricke, the poore boy is blind, and out of his best wit.

He will call himselfe home one day.

I shall be very glad for his sake truly.

I retire into the Citie, for we haue bene too long in this place.

Let vs go to Powles to see the Antiquities.

Let vs go vp into the Quire.

Who is buried within this wall?

It is Seba king of the Saxons, who conquered this countrie of England.

See what a goodly toombe there is truly. Who is entombed here?

Iohn of Gant duke of Lancaster, and sonne to king Henrie the third.

See here his lance and his target of horne.

What Epitaph is this?

Of sir Philip Sidney, the peerelesse paragon of letters and arms.

Let vs read it I pray you.

England, Netherland, the Heauens, and the Arts,
The Souldiors, and the World, haue made six parts
Of the noble Sydney: for none will suppose,
That a small heape of stones can Sydney enclose.
His body hath England, for she it bred,
Netherland his blood, in her defence shed:
The Heauens haue his soule, the Arts haue his fame,
All Souldiors the greefe, the World his good name.

Tis great pitie of this yong gentlemans death.
He is dead, and it is too late to call him from the dead.[1]

Eliot's young man in love uses all the hackneyed epithets
of the Petrarchist and the sonneteer. He "plays the
Idolater". Names of mythological goddesses abound when
he is speaking of his mistress. Her physical charms are
described in the usual stock terms: eyebrows, vaults of
ebony; hair, gold wire; eyes, twinkling stars; lips, coral—
and so on. The "pratlers'" attitude to the poor lunatic
youth is one of benevolent pity and kindly hope that this
frenzy will soon pass. Immediately after this mild mockery
of the Petrarchist's hallucinations the name of Sir Philip
Sidney is introduced and the "pratlers" read his epitaph
in St Paul's.

Care must be exercised in drawing conclusions from
this passage because Eliot's dialogues are primarily parodies
of other dialogues. This last chapter of his follows fairly
closely Vives's *Garrientes* dialogue, in which a young man
in love, called Clodius, was introduced, and was said to be
writing verses to his mistress. This Clodius is evidently the
immediate ancestor of "Ieronimo Pierruche". Again,
when the "pratlers" look at the tombs in St Paul's, Eliot
is probably thinking of the Spanish-English dialogues of
William Stepney in which the speakers visit and describe
the interior of St Paul's. But Vives's description of the
lover is the merest fragment compared to Eliot's, and

[1] *Ortho-epia Gallica,* sigs. *v* 4, *x* 1, *x* 2: *Parlement of Pratlers,*
pp. 108–10.

Stepney does not mention Sir Philip Sidney's tomb. Therefore, although allowance must be made for the Vives and
Stepney themes, I think that Eliot also intended to recall
here the Petrarcan and anti-Petrarcan argument which
had raged round Sidney and to which Florio had alluded
in the *Second Fruits*.

We thus find that the Florio-Eliot controversy includes
a kind of garbled memory of Bruno, Sidney, "Stella" and
the love and anti-love dispute. The student of Italian and
French language manuals in the fifteen-nineties found himself willy nilly considering the question of to love or not
to love, to write sonnets or not to write sonnets.

*   *   *   *

The allusions in *Love's Labour's Lost* to stars, moons,
eyes, lights, darkness—allusions which have been explained
as references to the scientific studies of the "School of
Night"—are nearly always doubled by some comparison
with women's eyes, their bright glances, the powerful influences which stream from them.

> My love, her mistress, is a gracious moon,
> She, an attending star, scarce seen a light.[1]

So says Navarre speaking of the Princess of France and
of Rosaline, one of her attendant ladies. And again, when
he is addressing the ladies in their masks he says,

> Vouchsafe bright moon, and these thy stars to shine—
> Those clouds removed—upon our watery eyne.[2]

The whole theme of Berowne's great speech, which is the
key to the play, is to contrast the study of women's eyes
with the study of books, and to maintain that truth is
revealed in the former rather than in the latter.

To me, the answer to this riddle is now partially visible.
The conflict in the play between the study of eyes, stars,

[1] IV. iii. 226–7.   [2] V. ii. 205–6.

lights, and the study of the light in ladies' eyes reflects the reproaches addressed to Sidney by Bruno for wasting his time over "Stella's" eyes instead of pursuing the light of knowledge.[1] The "stars" are the scientific, astronomical and mathematical studies of the Raleigh group, the formation of which was powerfully influenced by Bruno, and the "eyes" are the life of real earthly experience, as typified in the star-like eyes of "Stella" which Bruno tried to teach Sidney to despise.

But did Shakespeare know enough Italian to read the *Eroici Furori* dedication which has never been translated into English? Possibly not, but that does not affect the issue in the least. Shakespeare obtained this theme from the source, or rather sources, which we have been demonstrating throughout as the key to this play—namely Florio's and Eliot's language-dialogues. He took the "Venetia" proverb from the *Second Fruits* collection of travel-proverbs. Did he not also look at the much more fascinating collection of love-proverbs in the same book? Once started on that he would plunge into the atmosphere of stars and night in which it was framed, and any contemporary would explain to him that it referred to an Italian philosopher called Bruno who had held strange views about the stars and other matters and had made curious comments upon the late Sir Philip Sidney's famous romance with the lovely Lady Rich. All this would help him to understand more clearly the *Astrophel and Stella* sonnets, the clandestine publication of which in the same year as the *Second Fruits* caused much stir, and started the craze for sonnet-writing of which he himself was to be the most magnificent exponent.

He would notice in Florio's dialogue the parallel presentation of the Petrarcan and the anti-Petrarcan themes, and in Eliot's reply to Florio the amusing mockery of the

[1] The *Eroici Furori* dedication is really a reproach, in spite of the superficial exemption of English "stars" from blame.

exaggerations of the Petrarchist. Or perhaps these influences came to him not so much from the printed texts,
which are all we have to go upon, as from the actual
conversation of the men themselves. Be that as it may,
the presentation of the Petrarcan and the anti-Petrarcan
arguments is a most noticeable feature of *Love's Labour's
Lost*. The play might almost be called an essay on the subject
of sonnet-writing. Berowne starts as a pronounced anti-
Petrarchist. He is not an ascetic and is most reluctant to
take the vows proposed by the others. He is famous for
his contemptuous and mocking attitude to women. When
he falls in love with Rosaline he realises with horror what
a total reversal of his principles this involves.

> And I—
> Forsooth in love, I that have been love's whip!
> A very beadle to a humorous sigh,
> A critic, nay, a night-watch constable,
> A domineering pedant o'er the boy,
> Than whom no mortal so magnificent—
> This wimpled, whining, purblind, wayward boy,
> This Signior Junior, giant-dwarf, Dan Cupid,
> Regent of love-rhymes, lord of folded arms,
> Th'anointed sovereign of sighs and groans,
> Liege of all loiterers and malcontents,
> Dread Prince of Plackets, King of Codpieces,
> Sole imperator and great general
> Of trotting paritors—O my little heart!
> And I to be a corporal of his field,
> And wear his colours like a tumbler's hoop...
> What I! I love! I sue! I seek a wife!
> A woman, that is like a German clock,
> Still a-repairing, ever out frame,
> And never going aright, being a watch,
> But being watched that it may still go right.
> Nay, to be perjured, which is worst of all;
> And among three to love the worst of all—
> A whitely wanton with a velvet brow,

With two pitch-balls stuck in her face for eyes,
Ay and, by heaven, one that will do the deed,
Though Argus were her eunuch and her guard!
And I to sigh for her, to watch for her,
To pray for her, go to: it is a plague
That Cupid will impose for my neglect
Of his almighty dreadful little might...
Well, I will love, write, sigh, pray, sue, and groan—
Some men must love my lady, and some Joan.[1]

These are the coarse insinuations of the anti-Petrarchist,
his disbelief in the legend of women's inaccessibility and
chastity, his proverbs against women. "A woman is like
a German clock" is just the kind of proverbial remark
which Florio puts into the mouth of his anti-Petrarchist,
Pandolpho.

It is and euer was a womans fashion,
To loue a crosse, to crosse a louing passion.
And therefore are they compared to death, who
Followes those that flie her, and shunneth those that ply her.
To Nettles: Those that but touch they sting them,
But hurt not those that wring them. They are like Cocodrills,
They weepe to winne, and wonne they cause to dye,
Follow men flying and men following flye.
Like the ballance, where most it receiueth, there most it
    inclineth,
Like to a coale, which either burneth, or besmeareth.
Or like a wind-mill, which still doth go, as the wind doth blow.[2]

Berowne now praises, now blames Cupid. So do Florio's
speakers now derive Love's descent from idleness and beg-
gary, now exalt him as "Dictator" and "Dominus":

Siluestro. You runne wide Sir, Loue is the grandchilde of
nature, and first borne of beautie, by her husband pleasure.

Pandolpho. There lay a straw, for you shoote wide, hold your
hand a while, his grandame was idlenes (as Seneca saies) his
mother beggerie, as Plato tells vs, his father Herebus, as Lucian
reporteth, or Argus as Sir Philip Sidney declareth in drawing of

[1] III. i. 172–204.   [2] *Second Fruits*, sig. Z 4.

his pedegree; or God knowes who, for who els knowes who hath priuate in the common.

Siluestro. Nay if names beare games. Loue is the keykeeper of the world, as Orpheus saies, not onely the auncientest, as Hesiodus shewes, but euen the God of Gods, as good Tasso setts downe in his creede: taking from Mars his sword, from Neptune his trident, and from Iupiter his thunderbolt, and (if I misse not my mark) from Homer his verse, and from Hercules his club. So like a Dictator he is *Dominus fac totum*, and who but he? Like Plato banishing both mine and thine out of his Commonweale....[1]

Berowne's mention of Cupid and Argus also reminds one that Florio speaks of Sir Philip Sidney's having traced Cupid's descent from Argus, alluding to a poem in the *Arcadia*.[2]

The corner-stone of the play is the great scene in which the men come in one by one and read their sonnets whilst the mocking Berowne is concealed in a tree and overhears them all. His comments in his concealment are characteristic. He makes the anti-Petrarchist point that the abject worship of women as goddesses is idolatrous.

> A woman I forswore, but I will prove,
> Thou being a goddess, I forswore not thee,[3]

sighs Longaville, and Berowne comments,

> This is the liver-vein, which makes flesh a deity,
> A green goose a goddess—pure, pure idolatry.
> God amend us, God amend, we are much out o'th'way.[4]

So does Florio's Siluestro babble of goddesses, of Minerva, of Diana, of Ceres, and is rebuked by Pandolpho's remark,

> The best is, your creede is not sung in the church, neither doth your voyce enter heauen gates, nor shall they enter my head or Creede. I beleeue in GOD and not in women....[5]

[1] *Second Fruits* sig. Y4.
[2] Sir Philip Sidney, *Complete Works*, ed. A. Feuillerat, I, 239.
[3] IV. iii. 62–6.   [4] IV. iii. 72–4.   [5] *Second Fruits*, sig. Aa2.

But Berowne has no right to jeer at his friends for he also has succumbed to the power of women's eyes and when he is at last found out it is he who gives the supreme utterance to the play's thesis of the supremacy of love as the only revelation of reality.

> O, we have made a vow to study, lords,
> And in that vow we have forsworn our books;
> For when would you, my liege, or you, or you,
> In leaden contemplation have found out
> Such fiery numbers as the prompting eyes
> Of beauty's tutors have enriched you with?
> Other slow arts entirely keep the brain;
> And therefore, finding barren practisers,
> Scarce show a harvest of their heavy toil.
> But love, first learnéd in a lady's eyes,
> Lives not alone immuréd in the brain;
> But with the motion of all elements,
> Courses as swift as thought in every power,
> And gives to every power a double power,
> Above their functions and their offices.
> It adds a precious seeing to the eye;
> A lover's eyes will gaze an eagle blind;
> A lover's ear will hear the lowest sound,
> When the suspicious head of theft is stopped;
> Love's feeling is more soft and sensible
> Than are the tender horns of cockled snails;
> Love's tongue proves dainty Bacchus gross in taste.
> For valour, is not Love a Hercules,
> Still climbing trees in the Hesperides?
> Subtle as Sphinx, as sweet and musical
> As bright Apollo's lute, strung with his hair;
> And, when Love speaks, the voice of all the gods
> Make heaven drowsy with the harmony.
> Never durst poet touch a pen to write,
> Until his ink were temp'red with Love's sighs;
> O, then his lines would ravish savage ears,
> And plant in tyrants mild humility.[1]

[1] IV. iii. 315-46.

"Love takes from Homer his verse, and from Hercules his club" says Florio's Siluestro. It is a far cry from this business-like presentation of the argument in tabular form for the convenience of those who would embrace the language of the muses to the splendour of such lines as

> For valour, is not love a Hercules,

and,

> Never durst poet touch a pen to write

but the idea in both is precisely the same. Siluestro collects and presents as raw material the stock allusions which Berowne transmutes into poetry. Florio's handy little collection of pro-love and anti-love arguments was, in my opinion, undoubtedly used by Shakespeare both in this play and in others.

The fascination of Florio's love-dialogue is that his somewhat commonplace, cut-and-dried treatment of the eternal theme of poets has behind it the shadow of personalities greater than his own. When Siluestro speaks of that "celestiall loue" described by Plato, his words contain a memory of Giordano Bruno, and of the burning words in which he had described the Platonic vision. And I believe that Shakespeare was not only familiar with Florio's love-dialogue but that he also had some idea of the history behind it, in short that there *are* traces of Bruno in *Love's Labour's Lost*.

The moment in the play at which "Berowne" is made to rhyme with "moon" is not without significance. It occurs at one of the times when the Princess of France is called a moon and her ladies, of whom Rosaline is one, stars.

> *King.* What zeal, what fury hath inspired thee now?
> My love, her mistress, is a gracious moon,
> She, an attending star, scarce seen a light.
> *Berowne.* My eyes are then no eyes, nor I Berowne.... [1]

[1] IV. iii. 225–8.

"Inspired fury" is no bad translation of "Eroici furori" and we have seen how the Diana-and-stars sonnet, which Bruno prefixed to that work, was echoed by Florio and applied by him to Lady Rich. These lines are, in my opinion, an undoubted allusion to Bruno. Moreover, the whole anti-Petrarchist attitude of Berowne in the play, which he later abandons for a hymn to love as the only reality, recalls the paradox of Bruno's position. Berowne's great speech with its hint of Pythagorean "numbers" and the music of the spheres, to me suggests some kind of vague acquaintance, probably at second or third hand, with the *Eroici Furori* dialogues.

Is it true, then, that Berowne *is* Bruno? I believe that his name and some of his characteristics—notably his use of astronomical metaphors, his combination of anti-Petrarcan woman-hating with a lofty philosophy of love—were deliberately meant to recall Bruno to the audience. But Berowne is certainly not Bruno as he actually was. In the first place, Shakespeare had not sufficient knowledge to construct such a portrait, having only a kind of garbled legend of one aspect of Bruno's life in London, and that not the most important, to go upon. There is no trace in Berowne of that philosophic thirst for the One, that all-absorbing passion for knowledge which might lead to that end, which was the mainspring of Bruno's life. Berowne understands love simply as physical love and his neo-Platonic language describes what is, quite frankly, a physical exhilaration. He is not torn between a theoretical belief in the spirituality of matter and a practical difficulty in relating material to spiritual experience, as Bruno was. Berowne's vindication of physical love may be an answer to Bruno or a misunderstanding of Bruno; but in any case Berowne *is* not the real Bruno.

I have said that Berowne's name recalled Bruno to the audience. But this name is generally interpreted as derived from the Maréchal Biron and as being, like Navarre,

Dumaine, Longaville, and so on, one of the "French news" names with which the play abounds. Is it possible to reconcile two such conflicting views of the meaning of the name? I believe that Thomas Nashe gives us, not exactly a clear answer to this question, but a hint that an answer existed. In the preface to the second edition of *Christs Teares*, published in 1594, Nashe complains that a number of busy wits have been looking for personal and topical allusions in his *Jack Wilton* or *The Unfortunate Traveller*. Nashe had talked much in *The Unfortunate Traveller* of the drunkenness and stupidity of the students at the university of Wittenberg. The "busy wits" have explained this as an attack on English universities. The simplest remark is suspected by them of having a double meaning.

> Let one but name bread, they will interpret it to be the town of Bredan in the low countreyes; if of beere he talkes, then straight he mocks the Countie Beroune in France.[1]

Here, then, is Nashe associating this name Beroune or Berowne with talk of beer and drinking and particularly of drunkenness and stupidity at universities.

Bruno had aroused much excitement by his attacks in the *Cena* on the stupidity of English doctors, and how they knew more about beer than about Greek. I suggest therefore that this name Berowne, derived from "French news", had in the circle for which Nashe and Shakespeare wrote some other associations, perhaps connected with the memory of Bruno's attack on the English universities. It is probably also significant that Chapman afterwards made such great use of the same name.

There are doubtless other elements in Berowne; it is probably not incorrect to associate him with Essex, as we shall see later. As I have frequently had occasion to remark,

---

[1] Nashe, *Works*, ed. R. B. McKerrow, II, 182.

the finding of "originals" for Shakespearean characters is not a satisfactory proceeding. The artist must use his experience as the raw material for his creation, but out of it he *creates*, that is to say he makes something new. The situation which I have tried to outline was, I believe, a part of Shakespeare's experience, but the use which he made of that experience remains a mystery. Berowne would not be what he is if Bruno had not spent two years in London and fired Shakespeare's imagination with the legend which he left behind him, but Berowne *is* Berowne, and no one else.

*   *   *   *

The history behind Florio's love-dialogue includes memories, not only of Bruno, but also of Sidney and "Stella". To understand the dialogue, some knowledge of *Astrophel and Stella*, as well as of the *Eroici Furori*, was necessary. Shakespeare had an inkling, probably at second hand, of the *Eroici Furori*. But he would not have to depend on others for his knowledge of Sidney's sonnets. He is practically certain to have read and re-read *Astrophel and Stella* with the greatest care. The romantic figure of Sidney, who was not long dead when Shakespeare first came to London, must have left its mark upon the dramatist's imagination, and the poet and sonneteer must surely have been intensely interested in the craftsmanship of Sidney's sonnets which were the first and—except Shakespeare's own—the most famous of the great Elizabethan series. I believe that distinct traces of Shakespeare's interest in *Astrophel and Stella* can be detected in *Love's Labour's Lost*.

A good many of the points made in Shakespeare's play are also made in Sidney's sonnets. There is the question of the poet's use of language and the poet's training. Like Shakespeare, Sidney has his hit at current literary affectations,

the elaborations of dainty wits who enamel with pied
flowers their thoughts of gold, the strange similes

>Of herbes or beastes which Inde or Afrike hold[1]

which enrich the lines of euphuists. This bizarre borrowed
wealth costs too dear for Sidney and he attempts no more
than to copy Nature.

>...in Stella's face I reed
>What Love and Beautie be; then all my deed
>But copying is, what in her Nature writes.[2]

The fifteenth sonnet has a similar theme. Sidney addresses
the imitators of Petrarch and reiterates that his inspiration
is not a borrowing from others but drawn direct from
Nature as exemplified in Stella's face. Similarly, in the
first sonnet he describes how he at first turned over the
leaves of others' compositions, studying their fine inventions, in order to find out how to express himself. But

>Invention, Nature's child, fled step-dame Studie's blowes[3]

and at last he realised that others could not help him and
that he must write directly from his own experience.

>Foole, said my Muse to me, looke in thy heart, and write.[4]

This is, in essence, the same argument as that developed
in *Love's Labour's Lost*. The play mocks the unoriginal
phrase-maker, the euphuist, the Petrarchist, and finally
forswears the

>Taffeta phrases, silken terms precise,
>   Three-piled hyperboles, spruce affectation,
>Figures pedantical—[5]

which fashion demanded. Nature, not Art, must be the
poet's inspiration and he must look in his heart to write.

>Never durst poet touch a pen to write,
>Until his ink were temp'red with Love's sighs.

[1] Sonnet III, l. 8.   [2] *Ibid*. ll. 12–14.
[3] Sonnet I, l. 10.   [4] *Ibid*. l. 14.   [5] v. ii. 406–8.

Moreover, as in Shakespeare's play, so in Sidney's sonnets, the conflict between Art and Nature goes deeper than the matter of literary style. It involves also a conflict between philosophical studies and the study of the sweet world, between heavenly Platonic illumination and the earthly light in Stella's eyes, between learning and love. Sidney who rather wished to "reach the fruite of Nature's choisest tree" or "seek heav'n's course or heav'n's inside to see" is drawn from his study by the force of Stella's eyes. So are the men in *Love's Labour's Lost* deflected from their studious intentions by the eyes of the Princess of France and her ladies. But whereas they find their true illumination in earthly love and so resolve the conflict, Sidney, in the sonnets at least, cannot reach that solution. He can never feel that his love for Stella is *right*, morally and spiritually as well as physically, and he seems only able finally to reach his peace by the rejection of the earthly love for the ideal and philosophical love.

> Leave me, O Love, which reachest but to dust;
> And thou, my mind, aspire to higher things.

There is a certain occasional similarity in the imagery in which this problem is presented in Shakespeare's play and in Sidney's sonnets. It has been emphasised again and again that the heavenly bodies, stars and moon, terms connected with light, darkness, day, night, eyes, seeing, and so on, constantly recur in the play in connection both with the men's studies and with their loves. This kind of imagery is also most characteristic of Sidney's sonnets which are throughout in keeping with the name "Stella" which he gives to Lady Rich. He speaks with curiosity and wonder of

> those lampes of purest light—
> Whose numbers, waies, greatnesse, eternitie,
> Promising wonders, wonder do invite,[1]

[1] Sonnet XXVI, ll. 2–4.

and compares them to "those two starres in Stella's face".
The starry nymphs in Diana's train are huntresses like
their mistress.

> Dian, that faine would cheare her friend the Night,
> Shewes her oft, at the full, her fairest face,
> Bringing with her those starry nimphs, whose chace
> From heavenly standing hits each mortall wight.[1]

Stella's eyes do move the spheres of beauty, they dart down
their rays, they are majestic and sacred lights. It is thus
evident that the astronomical metaphor is characteristic of
Astrophel and Stella as well as of *Love's Labour's Lost*.

It is also rather curious to notice that "Stella" had black
eyes and so had Rosaline, one of the "stars" in *Love's
Labour's Lost*. Both Berowne and Sidney feel that such
an unpopular colour requires some apology.

> When Nature made her chiefe worke, Stella's eyes,
> In colour blacke why wrapt she beames so bright?
> Would she, in beamie blacke, like painter wise,
> Frame daintiest lustre, mixt of shades and light?
> Or did she else that sober hue devise,
> In object best to knit and strength our sight;
> Least, if no vaile these brave gleames did disguise,
> They, sunlike, should more dazle then delight?
> Or would she her miraculous power show,
> That, whereas blacke seemes beautie's contrary,
> *She even in blacke doth make all beauties flow?*[2]

Thus Sidney. And Berowne also thinks that Rosaline's
darkness makes dark seem light.

> Devils soonest tempt, resembling spirits of light.
> O, if in black my lady's brows be decked,
>   It mourns that painting and usurping hair
> Should ravish doters with a false aspéct;
>   *And therefore is she born to make black fair.*[3]

Stella makes all beauties flow in black; Rosaline is born to
make black fair. This seems rather a coincidence. But

[1] Sonnet XCVII, ll. 1–4.   [2] Sonnet VII, ll. 1–11.   [3] IV. iii. 253–7.

Rosaline differs from Stella in having black hair as well as black eyes. It appears that Lady Rich's colouring was that striking and unusual combination of dark eyes and fair, or ruddy, hair.

Finally I would draw attention in this connection to the Russian masque in the play. When the men fall in love and abandon their studies for the pursuit of the ladies, they call upon the latter and start their courtship disguised as Russians or "Muscovites". The appearance of the men in Russian disguise characterises the moment in which love finally triumphs and draws Navarre and his friends away from their former preoccupations. These preoccupations are, however, recalled in the conversation about the "numbering" and "measuring" of many miles to which allusion has already been made. But the numbering and measurement of astronomical bodies is now abandoned for the study of another moon and other stars, the ladies, who are asked to remove their masks in these words:

> Vouchsafe bright moon, and these thy stars to shine—
> Those clouds removed—upon our watery eyne.[1]

Then music plays—earthly music, not the music of the spheres—and they tread a dancing "measure" with their human moon and stars.

The Russian masque in *Love's Labour's Lost* has exercised the critics considerably. The use of Russian costume at one of the Gray's Inn Revels is certainly significant as we shall see later. But I think that the following is also significant. I do not know whether anyone has ever drawn attention in this connection to certain lines in the second sonnet of the *Astrophel and Stella* sequence.

> Not at the first sight, nor with a dribbèd shot,
> Love gave the wound, which, while I breathe, will bleed;
> But knowne worth did in mine of time proceed,
> Till by degrees it had full conquest got.

[1] v. ii. 205–6.

> I saw, and liked; I liked, but lovèd not;
> I loved, but straight did not what Love decreed:
> At length, to Love's decrees I, forc'd, agreed,
> Yet with repining at so partiall lot.
> Now, even that footstep of lost libertie
> Is gone; *and now, like slave-borne Muscovite,*
> *I call it praise to suffer tyrannie;*
> And now employ the remnant of my wit
> To make me selfe beleeve that all is well,
> While, with a feeling skill, I paint my hell.

At the moment when Sidney finally succumbs to Stella's complete domination over him he calls himself a "slave-borne Muscovite". At the moment when Navarre and his men finally put themselves in the power of the ladies they come disguised as "frozen Muscovits", to pay their respects and worship "like savages" before them. It seems to me that Sidney's sonnet may be one explanation of the Muscovite masque in this play.

Another point which bears this out is that when the men appear in their Russian disguise the first words uttered after their arrival, by their spokesman Moth, are:

> 'All hail, the *richest* beauties on the earth'—

to which Boyet rejoins,

> Beauties no *richer* than *rich* taffeta.[1]

He is alluding to the masks which hide the ladies' faces. But here is "rich, richer, richest", all crammed into two lines, one of which is the opening line of a poem or sonnet to the ladies which Moth is trying to recite. When one remembers how Sidney played on the word "rich", meaning Rich, Stella's hated married name, this is surely somewhat significant. There are other occasions in the

---

[1] v. ii. 158–9. The "tears", "glasses", and "coaches" of Navarre's sonnet in iv. iii. 24–41 have been compared by J. M. Purcell (*Philological Quarterly*, 1931, x, 399) to similar metaphors in Sonnet cv of the *Astrophel and Stella* sequence.

play where the word "rich" is worked in rather significantly and which will be quoted later.[1]

The echoes of Bruno, the stars and the moon, and the love and the anti-love arguments thus travel to Shakespeare *via* Sidney and "Stella" as well as *via* Florio. For, with the insight of a contemporary, he would recognise Bruno's influence in *Astrophel and Stella* as well as in the *Second Fruits*.

*   *   *   *

I suggest, therefore, that a rumour of Bruno's arguments with Sidney on love and sonnet-writing is to be detected in *Love's Labour's Lost*. This is very closely allied to the "School of Night" interpretation of the play owing to the similarity between Bruno's attitude and that of the members of the Raleigh group. A part of the significance of the contrast in the play between the study of stars and the study of ladies' eyes is thus to be sought in the arguments by which Bruno tried to dissuade Sidney from sonnet-writing and which are reflected in Sidney's sonnets themselves. The black eyes of "Stella", and of Rosaline, thus become a kind of symbol of the powers of life ranged against the "artists". And let us not forget that Lady Rich was the sister of the Earl of Essex, and so at the very heart of the group for which this play seems to have been written.

The path which started with Florio and Eliot led through Harvey and Nashe to Chapman and the "School of Night". The path which started with Florio and Bruno has led to the same goal, and in so doing has already partially explained the antithesis in *Love's Labour's Lost* between the study of astronomy and the writing of sonnets to ladies' eyes.

---

[1] Mr Hoyt H. Hudson has brought together, in the article already referred to, numerous examples of punning on Lady Rich's name by contemporary poets. Sidney was very far from being the only one of her admirers to do this. In 1597 Gervase Markham, for example, addressed her as "thou rich, *Rich*, richest" which might almost be an echo of Moth and Boyet. See p. 173, note.

The Florio-Eliot clue has certainly justified itself as the right one with which to begin the unravelling of this play.

The prominence of Florio all the way along the second line of approach is impressive. In the earlier chapters he figured merely as one of an unpopular group of manual-writers; but now he has become more important. A character in the comic underplot may quote a proverb from his travel-dialogue, but the characters of the main plot are saturated in the atmosphere of his love-dialogue. All the anti-woman proverbs, the pro-woman mythology, the whole sonnet-writing theme recalled Florio as much as it did Bruno or Sidney for his *Second Fruits* was designed for the use of poets who would embrace the new sonneteering fashion. It was he who had perpetuated the Bruno legend, revived the anecdotes of Bruno's London life, brought the whole Bruno-Sidney-"Stella" story into the language-dialogues and so made it one of the points which Eliot answered. The Florian title of the play now has a new significance, for it was indeed odd that he who in the *First Fruits* had thought it labour lost to speak of love should in his second manual have provided so amply for the needs of those who wished to discourse on that very subject. And we also now begin to see why it was that Holofernes regarded himself as *the* authority on the sonnet.

Let me supervise the canzonet. Here are only numbers ratified, but for the elegancy, facility, and golden cadence of poesy, caret: Ovidius Naso was the man. And why, indeed, "Naso", but for smelling out the odoriferous flowers of fancy, the jerks of invention?[1] When the Italian's pupils wrote verses in praise of him they could rarely resist a pun on "Florio" and "flower".[2]

[1] IV. ii. 127–32.

[2] *John Florio*, pp. 54, 130–1. Samuel Daniel wrote the following lines in Florio's manuscript collection of proverbs:

"Italicos poterit flores cum nectere Florus,
    Nomine Florus, erit re quoqu; Florilegus,
Floribus ex istis (mirum) nasutus odores
    Non capit, at naso qui caret, ille capit."

Here we have "caret, naso, nasutus, flores, odores, Florio".

CHAPTER VII

The Earl of Northumberland and "Stella's" Sister

The "School of Night" had several aristocratic members besides Raleigh. Chapman mentions three of them, Northumberland, Derby and Carey, in his dedication to the *Shadow of Night*. How illuminating it would be if we could enter the mind of one of these three men, could hear him speak about his enthusiasm for the new sciences, could know his views upon the controversy between love and learning, poetry and philosophy, human experience and knowledge in the abstract, "villanists" and "artists". Fortunately we are able to do this. For I have come across, in the Record Office, a manuscript copy (hitherto quite unknown and unregarded save for a brief entry in the Calendar of State Papers) of an essay by the Earl of Northumberland—one of the three mentioned by Chapman—on the subject of love versus learning. This document enables us to re-traverse the ground covered in the last two chapters by a slightly different route. It both confirms and sheds fresh light upon the conclusions already reached, and will be, I believe, regarded by Shakespearean scholars as of no small importance.

"Deep-searching" Northumberland, as Chapman calls him, was introduced to Hariot by Raleigh and became profoundly interested in the former's work. Northumberland was more of a dilettante than Raleigh and left no *magnum opus* to the world, but he is not without a memorial. His *Advice to his Son* has been edited by Dr G. B. Harrison[1] and Mr Mark Eccles announces that he has

---

[1] Henry Percy, ninth Earl of Northumberland, *Advice to his Son*, ed. G. B. Harrison, 1930.

found an essay by the earl on *Friends and Friendship*.[1] The discourse which I am about to describe has some affinity in style and arrangement with both these compositions. Evidently the earl had some propensity towards expressing himself in essay-writing and these and, possibly, other papers by him were doubtless passed from hand to hand among his friends and acquaintance.

The Record Office manuscript[2] is written in a neat secretary script and is endorsed, in another hand, "My lo. of Northumb." Neither hand is Northumberland's own. There is no title, but the official who calendared the document has supplied one which fits the theme with exactitude; "On the entertainment of a Mistress being inconsistent with the pursuit of Learning". It seems to be addressed, at the beginning at least, to an unnamed lady whom the author describes as "neerer to me then any" and for whom he had formerly entertained a passion which has now cooled owing to his engrossment in mathematical studies. He writes to explain in detail how this transformation took place.

"Be not impatient that yow have not the successe of my love" he begins with some complacency, addressing this lady who is nearer to him than any. He then appears to forget her existence as an individual and passes to a cynical review of the various methods of seduction best suited to the conquest of Woman in general.

I conceaved if shee were yonge and irresolute, kindnes, curtesie, love honorably professed, greate care without harshnes was meanes to insinuate a speciall likinge. . . . If religiousely disposed, then to remove those feares incident to sinne sometymes by reasons waggishly let slippe, other tymes by reasons more sowndly uttered, and if auriculer confession, pennance, and repentance will not give dispensation, yet the motion of the spirrit may serve for excuse. . . . Stories of tender harts begettinge ends praise worthy may sometymes mollefie a distasted humor to loves pleading.

[1] Mark Eccles, *Christopher Marlowe in London*, 1934, p. 161.
[2] See Appendix III, pp. 206–11.

Consumed with sensual passion, the whole force of his mind was bent upon these various stratagems which might help him to his purposes.

Tumblinge these conceites from corner to corner of my braynes, nothinge resting vndone but how to compownd a mixture fittest to purchase my idle determination, both I and my fancies walked in a Cirkell, the one about the Chamber, the other to the first period of obteininge vntill I grew giddie with thinckinge, and thinckinge gyddelie, made me gyddie in walkinge.

In this state of mind he turned for relief to certain books which lay scattered near him, seeking particularly for "*Tharcadia*, or bookes of the like subiecte" whereby he might learn to utter his "lethargious passions" in pleasing order. It was then, as he believed, that a destiny prepared from eternity to cross his desires, intervened. For as he tossed and turned among these books seeking what he required, he came across a mathematical treatise by an Arabic author of the name of Alhazen. Angrily he threw it from him, but as he did so it flew open,

perhaps by reason of a Stationers thred vncutt, yet superstitiouse in my religion that it was the spirrit that directed me by hidden and vnconceaveable meanes what was good for my purpose, with a discontented eye I beheld it where I perceaved a demonstration of the colours of the Raynebowe the cause of his arkednes.

Not much attracted at first by this subject and with his mind still full of his mistress, he began with a careless hand and a distracted thought to shift many leaves "looking uppon them with earnestnes in apparance, yet almost marking nothing". Presently, however, he came to a place where his eye fell upon a figure more irregular than the others. This aroused his curiosity slightly and he paused to mark what it imported. "There did I behold a demonstration declaring the hight of the aier with no small wonder, bycause it had ever bene taught me, *Nullum vacuum in rerum natura*." He then "unchained" his mind from its former preoccupations in order to follow the argument, but ever and again leaping from the demonstration to thoughts of his mistress and from his mistress to the demonstration, so that he understood neither rightly. In the midst of this great "strife of humors" he told himself at one moment that if he obtained his mistress first he could return afterwards to the pursuit of knowledge, at the next he saw that such interruption would mean loss of the "iewell of tyme" and the exchange of "light for darknes". Now he took up the book and discarded his mistress; now he shut the book and embraced the "conceites of her shadowe". Finally, deciding that the study of two or three pages would suffice to clear up the point which he did not understand, he resolutely gave his whole mind to the book, perusing it with attention and joying in the author's wit. Thus he was allured to look further into the proofs and so, being carried from proposition to proposition, was led to "the veary principles most simple of knowledge in generall".

His mistress now finally lost the battle and, compared to knowledge, appeared ugly and deformed indeed, "not that she was so amongest women", he kindly adds, "but in respect of knowledge, for nothinge is faire or fowle simply of it self but in respect". He then sums up his whole argument with a peroration upon the happiness and quietude of mind which the pursuit of knowledge brings and the miseries and torments attendant upon earthly loves; but remarks in conclusion that he will not go so far as to affirm that it is impossible to enjoy a mistress and learning at the same time, although "to gaine a Mistris with longe sute, mutch passion, and many delaies, and follow knowledge in his hight is impossible".

Such were the struggles through which a neophyte must pass before he could attain full initiation into the "School of Night". This most curious document betrays the influence of Thomas Hariot in every line. In his correspondence with Kepler during the years 1606 to 1608 Hariot discourses on the rainbow,[1] the fame of his views on which had reached the foreign scientist. In this same correspondence he cites "Alhazen" as one of his authorities,[2] and, as to the causes of refraction, affirms his belief in the theory of the vacuum, "where we still stick in the mud",[3] thus mentioning the difficulty also noted by Northumberland. Among Hariot's manuscripts there are several pages of figures and diagrams headed, at the top of each page, "Alhazen".[4] These are evidently notes which he made on reading Alhazen's book. This was also the book pondered over by the Earl of Northumberland and there can be no doubt that the experiences described in his essay reflect the absorption of the "wizard earl", as suspicious contemporaries called him, in his mathematical studies under the guidance of Hariot.

"Alhazen" was evidently one of the textbooks used for those studies. Hasan ibn Hasan, or Alhazen, was a celebrated Arabic mathematician of the eleventh century who made important advances in the study of optics. The book which the love-sick earl opened so carelessly was probably the Latin translation of his chief work, the *Opticæ Thesaurus*, published at Bâle in 1572. This book has an engraved frontispiece illustrating the subject. It represents a large harbour containing shipping. In the foreground some men are studying an astrolabe. On the far side of the harbour is a town upon which fall oblique rays from a large sun in the top right-hand corner. Behind the town rises an impressive mountain range wrapped in thunderously woolly clouds, and these are over-arched on the left by an enormous rainbow which is perhaps the most noticeable

[1] Henry Stevens, *Thomas Hariot and his Associates*, 1900, pp. 178–9. See also Marjorie Nicolson, "The 'New Astronomy' and English Literary Imagination" in *Studies in Philology*, July 1935, XXXII, 432.
[2] Stevens, *op. cit.* p. 179. [3] *Ibid., loc. cit.*
[4] British Museum, Additional MSS. 6789, ff. 415–23.

feature of the whole composition. Possibly it was this work of art (which reminds one of how much the interest of a man like Raleigh in Hariot's work was bound up with a practical concern for improving the science of navigation) which caught Northumberland's wandering eye.

Now it is obvious that Northumberland's essay emanates from the same school of thought as Chapman's dedication to the *Shadow of Night*, in which the earl is mentioned by name with so much approval. Chapman's dedication opens with a cry concerning the "exceeding rapture of delight" which the deep search for knowledge brings with it. Yet, in spite of the tremendous satisfaction which it brings, all men do not seek for knowledge and you may see, says Chapman, passion-driven men, reading but to curtail a tedious hour and using the wits which were given them for better purposes upon the fabrication of idle conceits, "idolatrous platts for riches". But the spleen with which he contemplates such frivolity is stayed when he remembers "how ioyfully oftentimes you reported vnto me, that most ingenious *Darbie*, deepe searching *Northumberland*, and skill-imbracing *heire of Hunsdon* had most profitably entertained learning in themselves, to the vitall warmth of freezing science".

The Earl of Northumberland's discourse on love and learning could be most accurately described in Chapman's very words. It is the history of the transformation of a passion-driven man, reading, or intending to read, the *Arcadia* and books of a like subject but to curtail a tedious hour, into the deep-searching student of Alhazen who leads him to the rapturous contemplation of knowledge in his height. There is, moreover, rather a curious verbal coincidence in both texts. When Northumberland is addressing the lady nearer to him than any whom he has now forsaken for learning, he reminds her of the various devices which he had formerly used in order to win her favours.

"The platts how disgested, how contrived, yow may remember, the inventions from what conceate they proceeded yow did see and weare sorry, my violent passion
yow were content to yeeld vnto out of necessitie, because
it was otherwise booteles." Thus both Chapman and
Northumberland use this word "platts" to describe the
valueless, time-wasting activities of the passion-driven man.
When we remember that Northumberland was seeking
Sidney's *Arcadia* as a guide to the expression of his "lethargious passions", and that Chapman describes the "platts"
as "idolatrous"—the usual reproach of the anti-Petrarchist
to the Petrarchist—it looks as though the "platts" of the
passion-driven man before his conversion to mathematics
were probably sonnets to his mistress.

Was this paper by the earl already circulating in a select
group before 1594 and did Chapman know of it when he
wrote his dedication? Or did the earl write his essay after
1594 and, knowing that the Chapman dedication emanated
from the "School of Night", use some ideas and phrases
from it? The latter is the more probable, for this reason.
The most natural explanation of the status of the lady
described by the earl as nearest to him of any would be
that she was his wife; and it appears that he did not marry
until about 1594.[1]

Almost from the first the marriage was unhappy. The
violent wrangles of the Earl and Countess of Northumberland were the talk of the town. Lord Henry Howard,
describing the relations between the pair in a letter to a

---

[1] G. Brenan, *History of the House of Percy*, 1902, II, 56, says that
the earl was married "about 1594". Burke, *Peerage and Baronetage*,
also dates the marriage in this year, but the *Dictionary of National
Biography* puts it in 1595. A good deal of mystery surrounds the
separation of Dorothy Devereux from her first husband, Sir Thomas
Perrot, whom she married clandestinely in 1583, and her second
marriage to the Earl of Northumberland which took place while
Perrot was still alive.

friend,[1] uses a phrase which strongly suggests that he had seen a copy of the earl's essay on love and learning. He thinks that the root of their incompatibility lay in the earl who was infected "by the distemper of an atheist, that, besides Raleigh's Alcoran, admits no principles". The witness of Howard's letter indicates that this essay had indeed had some publicity and was indeed addressed to the Countess of Northumberland.

The essay was, then, composed after the earl's marriage, but it would be useful to be able to date it more exactly than this. The Record Office document itself has no date in a contemporary hand upon it, but the Calendar of Domestic State Papers assigns it to the year 1604, with a query. It seems to me likely that it found its way into the State Papers rather later than this. When Northumberland was arrested after the Gunpowder Plot, search was made among his papers for evidence which might incriminate him, and this document was possibly one of those confiscated by the government. Although it contains no trace of treason, it might be thought suspicious on other counts. What were these reasons, sometimes waggishly let slip, sometimes soundly uttered, which could remove the fears incident to sin? This hint of blasphemy is followed by a hint of Romish practices, auricular confession, penance (Northumberland was a Catholic), and the writer turns from his folly, not at God's bidding, but as the result of some queer train of thought very reminiscent of "atheist" Raleigh and his associates. So might someone looking for evidence against Northumberland after 5 November 1605 have reasoned. But although this document probably came into government hands after that date, the original, of which it is a copy, may have been composed much

---

[1] *The Secret Correspondence of Sir Robert Cecil with James VI*, ed. D. Dalrymple, 1766, pp. 31–2. The letter is quoted by Dr G. B. Harrison in the introduction to his edition of Northumberland's *Advice to his Son*, pp. 19–21.

earlier. Dr G. B. Harrison has noted that the first part of Northumberland's *Advice to his Son*, written about 1596, is in a more fantastic and elaborate style than the second part, written in 1609.[1] It seems to me that the style of the essay on love and learning resembles that of the first part of the *Advice*, rather than the second, and if so it was perhaps composed at about the same time or a little earlier, and not so very long after the earl's marriage.

Who was this unfortunate Countess of Northumberland whose husband dealt her such a coldly calculated literary and scientific insult? She was Dorothy Perrot, *née* Devereux, *the sister of "Stella" and of the Earl of Essex*. So that the literary side of the insult actually had a personal application. In contemning "platts" to ladies, imitated from Sidney's work, Northumberland was contemning his sister-in-law's famous admirer. To one sister were addressed the *Astrophel and Stella* sonnets, full of the breath of romance and of poetry; to the other this cynical tirade by a mathematical misogynist. Was the earl's essay deliberately planned and circulated as a counterblast to the habit of circulating sugared sonnets, imitated from Sidney, among one's private friends? Was the treatment meted out to the two sisters a kind of personification of the question raised by Bruno of whether writing sonnets to women was not a waste of time when one might be pursuing knowledge in his height? "Stella's" lover, though assailed by doubts, had continued to write sonnets and arcadian romances. But the husband of "Stella's" sister came down heavily, unmistakably, and publicly on the other side. It is difficult to resist the conclusion that the Earl of Northumberland's attitude to his wife must have formed a first-class literary and social sensation.

Something, also, of a political importance was attached to it. For some of the disagreements between the earl and his wife arose from the fact that she was vehemently

[1] *Advice to his Son*, *ed. cit.*, Introduction, pp. 43–5.

devoted to the person and fortunes of her brilliant brother, the Earl of Essex, whilst he had no very high opinion of Essex, tended to think him a showy and dangerous fellow, and was bound by ties of common interests and long-standing friendship to Essex's rival, Sir Walter Raleigh. This gave rise to violent altercations in the Northumberland household. One such is vividly described in the letter from Howard to Bruce already mentioned. Northumberland told his wife that both he and all his friends would end their lives before her brother's great god (James of Scotland) should reign in England. She replied "that rather than any other than King James should ever reign in this place, she would rather eat their hearts in salt, though she were brought to the gallows instantly". This conversation is of much later date than we have assigned to the essay, but it illustrates how these two lashed one another into fury. There is no doubt that the countess was a woman of passionate temper endowed with a bitter, shrewish tongue, but her husband's essay on love and learning demonstrates how sorely she was tried. When she could endure the earl no longer (they were constantly being separated and reunited) she tended to return to the sympathy of her own family and to console herself with the society of her splendid brother and sister and their friends. One of these friends, the Earl of Southampton, sympathised with her very strongly. Early in 1597 there was an open quarrel between the Earls of Northumberland and Southampton.[1] This quarrel was "like to have proceeded to a duel, as it produced a challenge".[2] Various causes no doubt contributed to this outbreak—Northumberland's pride in his ancient, feudal name and contempt for newly rich families like the Southamptons, his association with Raleigh and distrust of Southampton's leader, Essex. But it is also hinted that the immediate cause of the

---

[1] C. C. Stopes, *Henry, Third Earl of Southampton*, 1922, pp. 102–3.
[2] Thomas Birch, *Memoirs of the Reign of Elizabeth*, II, 274.

outbreak was that Southampton had too openly taken the Countess of Northumberland's part against her husband.[1]

*   *   *   *

The theme of Northumberland's essay on the pursuit of learning is the theme of Shakespeare's play, reversed. Navarre, Berowne, and company start with learning and abandon it for love. Northumberland starts with love, or what he calls love, and abandons it for learning. They begin with serious studies, apparently of a mathematical and astronomical character, and pass from them to the writing of sonnets in praise of their mistresses. He begins with curiously contrived "platts" for winning women's favours, with efforts to utter his "lethargious passions" in some kind of arcadian order, and passes from this to a close application of his mind to Alhazen on light and on the theory of the rainbow. They cannot find true knowledge or any insight into the nature of reality in their books; but they do find it revealed in love, reflected in the eyes of women. He found nothing but utter confusion, darkness, and distress of mind in the love of women; but in following a close mathematical argument concerning the nature of light from proposition to proposition he reached at last the very principles most simple of knowledge in general and rested therein in quietude of mind and felicity of soul. The play answers the document, the document answers the play, point for point. The discovery of this essay seems to me to prove that the "School of Night" interpretation of *Love's Labour's Lost* is correct, except that the emphasis should be on Northumberland rather than on Raleigh.

The influence of Hariot is unmistakable in the Northumberland document. This bears out Miss Seaton, Dr Harrison and others who have seen traces of Hariot in the play.

[1] Brenan, *op. cit.* II, 68.

Look, for instance, at Berowne's speech in the first scene.

> Why, all delights are vain, but that most vain
> Which, with pain purchased, doth inherit pain—
> As painfully to pore upon a book,
>   To seek the *light* of truth, while truth the while
> Doth falsely blind the eyesight of his look:
>   *Light*, seeking *light*, doth *light* of *light* beguile:
> So ere you find where *light* in darkness lies,
> Your *light* grows dark by losing of your eyes.[1]

The word "light" is used seven times in five lines. Does not this suggest that the book over which Berowne's friends were poring was on the subject of light? Did not Northumberland pore over Alhazen on the rainbow and on the theory of the spectrum? Was not Hariot also a close student of this subject? A few lines later Berowne makes his reference to astronomers.

> These earthly godfathers of heaven's *lights*,
>   That give a name to every fixéd star,
> Have no more profit of their shining nights,
>   Than those that walk and wot not what they are.[2]

Hariot and his friends were much addicted to peering at heaven's lights. And here Hariot's close study of optics was of use in eventually (probably not until considerably later than the play) enabling him to construct "perspective trunks", which were a species of telescope. Alhazen's book is on optics and it contains directions for the manufacture of magnifying glasses, which perhaps accounts for some of Hariot's interest. The study of light is, of course, closely allied to the study of optics, and if there is one group of words in *Love's Labour's Lost* which is played upon and introduced into every kind of context even more constantly than the "light, dark, sun, moon, stars" group, it is the "eyes, eyesight, look" group. This play

[1] I. i. 72–9.   [2] *Ibid.* 88–91.

is full of eyes. Immediately following the "light" lines
of Berowne's speech, quoted above, are some "eye" lines.

> ...Your light grows dark by losing of your *eyes*.
> Study me how to please the *eye* indeed,
>   By fixing it upon a fairer *eye*,
> Who dazzling so, that *eye* shall be his heed,
>   And give him light that it was blinded by.[1]

There can be little doubt, I think, that one of the books
which the king and his court are studying at the commencement of the play is the *Opticæ Thesaurus* of Hasan
ibn Hasan or Alhazen. The fact that the Earl of Northumberland's studies had weakened his eyesight and made him
less skilful with his rapier[2] perhaps gave an added point
to "losing of your eyes".

The Earl of Northumberland's essay gives us the second
half of the answer to the stars-eyes, love-learning antithesis
in *Love's Labour's Lost*. The Countess of Northumberland
joins her sister, Lady Rich, as a lady whose eyes had been
slighted for stars. The argument between Bruno and Sidney
on the relative merits of distilling the elixir of one's brain
into sonnets to "Stella" or employing it in the pursuit of
knowledge finds its counterpart here in Northumberland's
rejection of "platts" to "Stella's" sister, imitated from
Sidney's *Arcadia*, in favour of the pursuit of knowledge
in its height *via* the study of the spectrum. These two
ladies were the sisters of the Earl of Essex and so the bright
particular stars of the group of which Southampton was
a member and for which *Love's Labour's Lost* was written.
It is thus most natural to find Shakespeare coming gallantly
to their defence against their detractors of the "School of
Night".

Here, then, at last, is the answer to the riddle which
lies at the heart of the play. This is why stars are never
mentioned without being paired with eyes; why the light

---

[1] I. i. 79–83.   [2] Brenan, *op. cit.* II, 67, note 3.

of heaven's glorious sun is not brighter than the sun-
beaméd eyes of ladies; why the numbers that Petrarch and
Sir Philip Sidney flowed in carry the day against the
"number" of Pythagoras.

> Nay, I have verses too, I thank Berowne—
> The *numbers* true, and were the *numb'ring* too,
> I were the fairest goddess on the ground...
> I am compared to twenty thousand fairs.[1]

> We *number* nothing that we spend for you—
> Our duty is so *rich*, so infinite,
> That we may do it still without accompt.[2]

> For when would you, my liege, or you, or you,
> In leaden contemplation have found out
> Such fiery *numbers* as the prompting eyes
> Of beauty's tutors have *enriched* you with?[3]

And we must remember that the comic fantastics and
pedants also deal in both kinds of "numbers". "Assist me
some extemporal god of rhyme, for I am sure I shall turn
sonnet",[4] cries Armado. "What, my soul, verses?" exclaims Holofernes on seeing Berowne's letter. This is largely
because the Bruno-Stella theme had percolated to Shakespeare *via* Eliot's and Florio's manuals.

The Earl of Northumberland rejected the *Arcadia*, but
Shakespeare studied it with the greatest care. Not only the
theme of *Astrophel and Stella* but also many of the themes
of the *Arcadia* and much of its language can be traced in
Love's Labour's Lost. There is no space here to work out
in detail these echoes. Some of them are hinted at in
various annotated editions of the play but the whole
question of Shakespeare's debt to the *Arcadia* ought to be
gone into more fully. Cleophila's curious "light-dark"
poem, in which the darkness of passion wars with the light

[1] v. ii. 34–7.   [2] *Ibid.* 198–200.
[3] IV. iii. 317–20.   [4] I. ii. 175–6.

of reason,[1] probably has something to do with the "light-dark" theme in *Love's Labour's Lost*, and there are many other interesting points of contact between Shakespeare's play and Sidney's novel. One of the main clues to the play is the fact that Shakespeare is there using allusions to the dead Sidney's work as a compliment to the living. Not only was *Astrophel and Stella* addressed to Lady Rich, but, if we are to believe Aubrey's friend Tyndale,[2] Pamela and her black-eyed sister Philoclea, who are the heroines of the *Arcadia*, were meant to represent the Countess of Northumberland and Lady Rich.

*   *   *   *

The Earl of Northumberland's essay is thus of vital importance to the understanding of the play and it links on quite logically to our earlier arguments. It is the third of the documents printed at the end of this book, and these are all three connected with one another. The description of Northumberland's transformation from a "passion-driven" into a "deep-searching" man is allied, primarily to Bruno's arguments with Sidney, and secondarily to Chapman's dedication to the *Shadow of Night*. The latter, in turn, is a reflex from the Eliot speech in *Pierces Supererogation* on "artists" of various varieties. Out of these three documents, when their history and implications are fully understood, can be woven an answer which covers most of the topicalities in this play, the jokes about brawling in French, charge-houses, piercing a hogshead, young Juvenal, *Venetia, Venetia*, labour lost to speak of love, the pedant with the Rabelaisian name, schools of night, chapmen, mathematics and multiplication, poets and astronomers, Berowne and moon, stars and eyes, sunlight and bright glances, Petrarcan and Pythagorean numbers, sonnets and ladies.

[1] Sir Philip Sidney, *Complete Works*, ed. A. Feuillerat, IV, 169.
[2] J. Aubrey, *Brief Lives*, ed. A. Clark, 1898, II, 250–1.

CHAPTER VIII

The Gray's Inn Revels

Shakespeare may have seen a copy of Northumberland's essay, but it is not absolutely essential to our argument to suppose that he did so. The essay is invaluable to us as an illumination of the attitude of one member of the "School of Night", but Shakespeare would not be in need of a written illumination, as we are, since he walked and talked daily with his contemporaries and knew what was being said and thought round about him. But whether or not Shakespeare saw this essay, his play reflected something of the situation which it describes and must therefore have been written (leaving revision out of the question for the moment) after Northumberland's marriage and after his disagreements with his wife had developed and become public.

According to Brenan, who is the chief authority on Northumberland, the earl's marriage took place "about 1594"[1] whilst his wife's first husband, Sir Thomas Perrot, was still alive. The date is, however, difficult to determine exactly in the absence of any definite record and, as Brenan says, the circumstances surrounding the marriage are mysterious. Did Dorothy Perrot, *née* Devereux, obtain a separation from her first husband before marrying Northumberland, or was her first marriage regarded as invalid? After she had become Countess of Northumberland she was involved in a lawsuit in trying to obtain possession of money settled upon her by Perrot, but Burleigh and Coke appear to have withheld her settlements, perhaps on account of some irregularity in her first marriage. Brenan says that

[1] *Op. cit.* II, 56.

this lawsuit was one of the subjects of contention between the earl and his wife, who were at loggerheads "almost from the first". They were separated four times during the first five years of married life.

Love's Labour's Lost and Northumberland's essay may therefore have been written any time after the unknown date in 1594 when Northumberland married "Stella's" sister. And it is my belief that the immediate inspiration of *both* the play *and* the essay was the Gray's Inn Revels of 1594–5.

It has already been urged by Sir Edmund Chambers[1] and, independently, by Mr Rupert Taylor,[2] that there is some connection between *Gesta Grayorum*[3] and *Love's Labour's Lost*. The members of Gray's Inn, led by their duly elected Lord of Misrule, or "Prince of Purpoole", revelled in their traditional manner on a grand scale during the Christmas season of 1594 and in the New Year of 1595 until Shrove Tuesday. A curious account of these revels is preserved in the work entitled *Gesta Grayorum*. Shakespeare is known to have been involved in these doings, for his *Comedy of Errors* formed the entertainment on 28 December, a crowded and confused evening which was afterwards known as the "Night of Errors". And we learn that on 3 January the company included, amongst others, the Earl of Northumberland, the Earls of Southampton and Essex, Lord Rich, and "a great number of Knights, Ladies and very worshipful Personages".[4] These names place us at once at the heart of the situation reflected in *Love's Labour's Lost*.

The Gray's Inn Revels, as described in *Gesta Grayorum*, are largely planned from what we have become accustomed to call, after Eliot, the "villanist" point of view. Amongst

---

[1] *William Shakespeare*, I, 335–6.
[2] *The Date of Love's Labour's Lost*, pp. 1–9.
[3] *Gesta Grayorum*, ed. W. W. Greg, Malone Society Reprints, 1914.
[4] *Ibid.* p. 25.

the rules governing the mock "Order of the Helmet" is the following:

Item, No Knight of this Order shall, in point of Honour, resort to any Grammar-rules out of the Books *De Dullo*, or such like; but shall, out of his own brave Mind, and natural Courage, deliver himself from Scorns, as to his own Discretion shall seem convenient.[1]

Yet the knights are advised and encouraged to undertake a little light reading, of works such as the *Arcadia* for instance, and to frequent the theatre.

Item, Every Knight of this Order shall endeavour to add Conference and Experience by Reading; and therefore shall not only read and peruse *Guizo*, the *French* Academy, *Galiatto* the Courtier, *Plutarch*, the *Arcadia*, and the Neoterical Writers, from time to time; but also frequent the Theatre, and such like places of Experience; and resort to the better sort of Ord'naries for Conference, whereby they may not only become accomplished with Civil Conversations, and able to govern a Table with Discourse; but also sufficient, if need be, to make Epigrams, Emblems, and other Devices appertaining to His Honour's learned Revels.[2]

Most sternly excepted from the general pardon granted by the Prince of Purpoole to his subjects are all those who fail in their duty to ladies.[3]

The general trend of *Gesta Grayorum* is, however, to be discerned most clearly in the speeches of the six counsellors who give sage advice to the Prince of Purpoole. The first urges him to seek fame and to eternise his name by war; the third suggests that fame is best acquired by the erection of great monuments and buildings. But the second counsellor advises the study of philosophy, "that you bend the Excellency of your Spirits to the searching out, inventing and discovering of all whatsoever is hid in secret in the World, that your Excellency be not as a Lamp that shineth

---

[1] *Gesta Grayorum*, p. 28.   [2] *Ibid.* pp. 29–30.   [3] *Ibid.* p. 16.

to others, and yet seeth not it self; but as the Eye of the World, that both carrieth and useth Light".[1] Towards the end of this speech "Trismegistus" is mentioned.

The sixth and last counsellor flatly contradicts the second and indeed all the other five. Is the prince then to spend all his time in labours like these? Is he to have no pleasure? "What!" he exclaims, "Nothing but Tasks, nothing but Working-days? No Feasting, no Musick, no Dancing, no Triumphs, no Comedies, no Love, no Ladies?"[2] Thus does the sixth counsellor "perswade Pass-times and Sports", and since his advice was the most suited to a time of revelry it was followed.

The next day the prince was visited by some mock ambassadors from Russia.[3] Just before the entry of the Russians there was a very stately masque and dance in which ladies took part. This visit of the imaginary Russians was later returned when the Prince of Purpoole himself went on an imaginary visit to that country whence he returned on 1 February with his health impaired by "Sickness at Sea".[4] The long period of revelling was finally closed by a masque which was given at court.

Quite clearly this light-hearted atmosphere of the Gray's Inn Revels is the atmosphere of *Love's Labour's Lost* with its dancing ladies and its mock Russians, at whom Rosaline hurls her taunt

Sea-sick, I think, coming from Muscovy.[5]

As Mr Taylor has pointed out,[6] this must certainly be an echo of *Gesta Grayorum*. Moreover, I think that it may be significant that the four men disguised as Russians in the play are described as "a mess of Russians".[7] According to the *Oxford English Dictionary* a "mess" which now

---

[1] *Gesta Grayorum*, p. 34.
[3] *Ibid.* pp. 44 ff.
[5] v. ii. 393.
[7] v. ii. 361.

[2] *Ibid.* p. 41.
[4] *Ibid.* pp. 54–5.
[6] *Op. cit.* pp. 8–9.

means a company of persons eating together originally
meant

each of the small groups, normally of four persons (sitting together
and helped from the same dishes), into which the company at a
banquet was divided. Now only in the Inns of Court, a party
of four benchers or four students dining together.

Probably the word "mess" meaning four persons was
already in Shakespeare's day rather particularly associated
with the Inns of Court, and the "mess of Russians" in
Love's Labour's Lost must have been a joke particularly
intended for the consumption of members of Gray's Inn
as a reminder of their recent revels. I believe that various
other jokes and allusions in the play may also be connected
with slang and customs current in Gray's Inn. And the
speeches of the counsellors in *Gesta Grayorum* are undoubtedly reflected in the first scene and first line of the
play:

> Let fame, that all hunt after in their lives,
> Live registred upon our brazen tombs.

The plan which the King of Navarre draws up at the
beginning of the play follows the advice of the second
counsellor. He will live in philosophy; he will seek the
light of truth and study things hid and barred from common
sense, and so achieve fame. Berowne's protest,

> O, these are barren tasks, too hard to keep,
> Not to see ladies, study, fast, not sleep,[1]

recalls the cheerful advice of the sixth counsellor, and in
the play, as in the revels, it is that advice which is eventually
taken.

The Earl of Northumberland, as well as Shakespeare,
heard those speeches at the Gray's Inn Revels, and if
Love's Labour's Lost is a development of the speech of the
sixth counsellor Northumberland's essay is a defence of

[1] I. i. 47–8.

the position of the second counsellor and a contradiction of the whole attitude of the revels. Frivolous reading of works such as the *Arcadia*, undertaken with a view to making oneself more agreeable in society, was advised by the revelling "Grayans" but is totally rejected by the earl in his essay. Like the second counsellor he believes in devoting himself to serious study, to the profound search for the light of truth, and in order to do this he discards all worldly dalliance.

It is my belief, therefore, that *Love's Labour's Lost* and the Earl of Northumberland's essay both took their immediate inspiration from the Gray's Inn Revels of 1594–5, Shakespeare being on the side of the "Grayans" whilst Northumberland is against them. The words in which the second counsellor advised the Prince of Purpoole to study philosophy and to become as "the Eye of the World, that both carrieth and useth Light" were thus approved by Northumberland and the "School of Night" who applied themselves to the scientific study of light, and reprobated by Berowne in Shakespeare's play.

> Light, seeking light, doth light of light beguile:
> So ere you find where light in darkness lies,
> Your light grows dark by losing of your eyes.

It is very curious indeed to remember that the speeches of the counsellors in *Gesta Grayorum* have been attributed to Francis Bacon,[1] and if that attribution is correct, and

---

[1] Spedding made the attribution on grounds of style and there is further evidence for it in the so-called "Northumberland" Manuscript in which the entry "Orations at Graies Inne reuells" seems to be classed with other works by Bacon. (See F. J. Burgoyne, *Collotype Facsimile and Type Transcript of an Elizabethan Manuscript*, 1904, p. xiii.) Another set of speeches by Bacon which was included in his collection by the person who compiled that manuscript also deals, in some degree, with the theme of love and learning and of reading to gain experience. (Burgoyne, pp. 55–62.) Bacon wrote these speeches for a masque presented to the Queen by the Earl of Essex in November 1595, and the soldier's speech was delivered by someone who had

I am also correct in hearing echoes of those speeches in *Love's Labour's Lost*, then the "civil war of wits" in that play may be, in one of its aspects, a reflection of some friendly crossing of swords between the two greatest wits of the age, Shakespeare and Bacon. Dr Caroline Spurgeon's recent comparison of Bacon's imagery with Shakespeare's[1] has shown that Bacon is constantly using "light" as an image of the mind and of the illumination which comes from knowledge, whilst with Shakespeare "light" seems to suggest "love". This line of thought seems to me one which it might be very interesting to pursue in connection with this play and its corollary, the Earl of Northumberland's essay.

I think that the reason why *Love's Labour's Lost* and the Northumberland essay both derive from the Gray's Inn Revels is because the revels themselves were planned by "villanists" against "artists", by the Essex group against the Raleigh group. The jests and the fooling of *Gesta Grayorum* read as though they were meant for certain people. The things which the Knights of the Helmet must not do or say sound like things which someone *had* done or said.

Item, that no Knight of this Order shall take upon him the Person of a Male-content, in going with a more private Retinue than appertaineth to his Degree, and using but certain special,

---

"played Pedantiq" at Cambridge. (Burgoyne, p. 56.) In this masque we are probably again close to the atmosphere in which *Love's Labour's Lost* was written. Indeed I think that a fuller working out of the connections between Northumberland's essay and *Gesta Grayorum* may eventually throw some light upon the principles which guided the selection of the pieces included in the "Northumberland Manuscript" and may even help to explain what was vaguely passing in the mind of the person who scrawled the names of Shakespeare and Bacon and (once) the word "honorificabiletudine", which is reminiscent of *Love's Labour's Lost*, all over its title-page.

[1] Caroline F. E. Spurgeon, *Shakespeare's Imagery and What it Tells Us*, 1935, pp. 16–29.

obscure Company, and commending none but Men disgraced, and out of Office; and smiling at good News, as if he knew something that were not true; and making odd Notes of His Highness's Reign, and former Governments; or saying, that His Highness's Sports were well sorted with a Play of Errors; and such like pretty Speeches of Jest, to the end that he may more safely utter his Malice against His Excellency's Happiness; upon pain to be present at all His Excellency's most glorious Triumphs.[1]

Was this aimed at the Earl of Northumberland, who consorted with the disgraced Raleigh, who kept company with the obscure "School of Night"? And had Northumberland criticised Shakespeare's *Comedy of Errors*?

The spirit of aristocratic faction lies at the back of the situation which we have been trying to explore. On the one hand are Raleigh, Northumberland and their friends who stand for obscure learning and science and a kind of contempt for social life and who are extolled by "artistic" poets such as Chapman. On the other hand are Essex, Southampton and their friends who typify elegance and grace and youth and *savoir vivre* and who have amongst them a tradition of poetry which derives from Sidney. Shakespeare was the poet of this group, and the young "Grayans" studied his beautiful language with admiration and strove to imitate his love-poetry. And the *Shadow of Night*, *Gesta Grayorum*, Northumberland's essay and *Love's Labour's Lost* were all in their way expressions of these rivalries.

* * * *

The "Grayans" had perhaps been provoked by the publication in 1594 of *Willobie His Avisa*[2] which Dr G. B. Harrison and others believe to have been an attack on the Essex-Southampton group inspired by the Raleigh group.

---

[1] *Gesta Grayorum*, p. 31.
[2] *Willobie His Avisa*, ed. G. B. Harrison, 1926.

The book contains one of the earliest mentions of Shake-speare's name.

> *Though* Collatine *haue deerely bought,*
> *To high renowne, a lasting life,*
> *And found, that most in vaine haue sought,*
> *To haue a* Faire, *and* Constant *wife,*
>   *Yet* Tarquyne *pluckt his glistering grape,*
>   *And* Shake-speare, *paints poore* Lucrece *rape.*
>
> *Though* Susan *shine in faithfull praise,*
> *As twinckling Starres in Christall skie,*
> Penelop's *fame though* Greekes *do raise,*
> *Of faithfull wiues to make vp three,*
>   *To thinke the* Truth, *and say no lesse,*
>   *Our* Auisa *shall make a messe.*

It is perhaps significant that Avisa makes up a "messe", or group of four, with Shakespeare's Lucrece, the star-like Susan, and Penelope. The emphasis on "Penelope" in *Willobie His Avisa* is rather interesting in view of the fact that the chief lady of the Essex-Southampton group was called Penelope Rich; and Shakespeare's "mess of Russians" in *Love's Labour's Lost* may include memories of Sidney's sonnets to "Stella", as already suggested, and of *Willobie His Avisa*, as well as of the Gray's Inn Revels. Those revels merely brought to a head a controversy which had been going on sporadically for some time. The young men of the Inns of Court knew all about the dispute between two aristocratic factions concerning the rival merits of com-posing sonnets to some "Stella" and studying the real stars in the Copernican heavens.

*   *   *   *

The young men of the Inns of Court were also given to the study of modern languages, and this brings us back again once more to the ubiquitous Eliot and Florio.

The education of the young Elizabethan of good birth was often completed, generally after having taken a degree at Oxford or Cambridge, at one of the Inns of Court. The revelling "Grayans" were thus really high-spirited young students. Law was, of course, their chief subject of study, but they were still putting a general "finish" to their education and they made use of the advantages which London offered as a centre for the study of modern languages. Miss Lambley points out that there were better facilities at the Inns of Court than at Oxford or Cambridge for the study of the tongues as Farringdon Without ward was a favourite abode of the French teachers.[1] De la Mothe was probably a teacher frequented by law students as his *French Alphabet* contains a disquisition on the differences between the French spoken in France and the law French of England.[2] Florio was also doubtless very well known to the Inns of Court students as the most celebrated of all the teachers of Italian. Such lively young men as were these students would much enjoy the general "ragging" of tutors and text-books which Eliot permitted himself in his *Ortho-epia Gallica.* The words of yet another language-teacher, John Minsheu, may be quoted here as proof of this. Minsheu brought out some Spanish-English dialogues in 1599 which he dedicated to the students of Gray's Inn. In his preface he seems rather afraid that he will be laughed at for his pains.

...if a man haue any learning or qualitie, let him bring it to you, and if it be too tedious vnto you, or hinder your sport, rather then be troubled with him, bob him or flout and scoffe him away. Be not imitators of *Demosthenes* which spent more

---

[1] K. Lambley, *The Teaching and Cultivation of the French Language in England*, 1920, p. 209.

[2] This may have something to do with the pun on "Moth" and "mote" in *Love's Labour's Lost.* At Gray's Inn the "Utter-Barresters" were set to practise their pleading on imaginary cases and questions which were called "Motes". The younger learners, or "Inner-Barresters" had to recite by heart afterwards the pleading of these "Mote-Cases" in Law-French. See W. R. Douthwaite, *Gray's Inn, its History and Associations*, 1886, pp. 31–2.

oyle in the lampe in studying to enrich his minde, then wine to comfort his bodie; but rather waste your wine and spare your candles....[1]

To me, this sounds as though Minsheu knew how much Gray's Inn had enjoyed the *Ortho-epia Gallica*. Curiously enough, too, one of the subscribers to Minsheu's *Ductor in Linguas* (1617) is described as "Henry the second Prince of Graya and Purpoole" which suggests some knowledge of the revels.

The drift of my argument here is that once again an already existing interpretation of the satire of *Love's Labour's Lost* endorses rather than contradicts my Eliot-Florio hypothesis. The play seems to have been designed for an audience which knew of the Gray's Inn Revels. Such an audience would also be very likely to know of, and to appreciate references to, Eliot's *Ortho-epia Gallica*.

* * * *

There is another line of argument which may not seem on the surface to be relevant but which really fits into place here; it is concerned with certain connections which are, I believe, to be discerned between *Ortho-epia Gallica* and *Willobie His Avisa*.

Eliot's *Ortho-epia Gallica* was published in the year before *Willobie* came out. The scene of one of Eliot's dialogues is laid at an inn. The inn scene was traditional in language dialogues and had been used by several of Eliot's predecessors, notably Hollyband. But in his usual "villanistic" manner Eliot introduces wickedness into the harmless inn scene by causing the guest to make love to Gaudinetta, the innkeeper's daughter, who escapes from him to her parents who are calling her away.[2] In the last of the *Ortho-epia* dialogues, which contains among other stories the description of the lovesick youth and of an

[1] See *John Florio*, pp. 172–3.
[2] *Ortho-epia Gallica*, sigs. q1, q2: *Parlement of Pratlers*, pp. 91–2.

alchemist, there is much talk of birds and of the song of birds. The tale of the competition between the cuckoo and the nightingale as to whose was the sweetest song is told in some detail. The song of the lark whose "tee-ree-lee-ree" is more melodious than all the tunes of Linus, Amphion, Orpheus or Arion, is listened to by the "pratlers" with great enthusiasm.[1] Some of these bird-allusions are suggested in the dialogue by Vives[2] which is one of the foundations of this dialogue of Eliot's, but the latter seems to develop the bird theme with rather special fervour. He also mentions, as Vives did not, the Greek comedy about birds by Aristophanes.

> Without doubt men haue learned Musicke of Birdes. Democritus vvas the Nightingales scholler, witnesse Aristophanes in his Comedie of the song of Birdes.[3]

The lark and nightingale stories are amongst the contents of his book mentioned by Eliot in one of his prefaces as being profound and deep mysteries.

> ...I haue written the whole booke in a merrie phantasticall vaine, and to confirme and stir vp the wit and memorie of the learner, I haue diuersified it with varietie of stories, no lesse authenticall then the deuises of *Lucians* dialogues: as of the Larke and her note of *Tee-ree-lee-ree*: the Nightingale and her *aubade*: the Spider and the Spideresse her daughter: the Seigneur *Valerian*, and his *beso las manos*: the terrible *Vespasian*, and his cutting and slashing: the Seignior *Cocodrill*, and his martiall Rhetoricke, with many other phantasticall plaisanteries to delight, not to dull your spirits. These are profound and deepe mysteries I may tell you, and verie worthie the reading, and such as I thinke you haue not had performed in any other boke that is yet extant.[4]

Willobie's "Avisa" was connected in some way with an inn. Moreover, it is, says Dr Harrison, "probable from

[1] *Ortho-epia Gallica*, sigs. *t2*, *t3*: *Parlement of Pratlers*, p. 104.
[2] Foster Watson, *Tudor School-boy Life*, pp. 45–6.
[3] *Ortho-epia Gallica*, sig. *v1*: *Parlement of Pratlers*, p. 106.
[4] *Ortho-epia Gallica*, sigs. B1 verso, B2: *Parlement of Pratlers*, p. 8.

the number of references to birds, falconers, lures, and so forth, that Avisa's name has some connection with a bird". I therefore suggest that Eliot's Gaudinetta, the inn-keeper's daughter, and his bird-allusions might conceivably throw some light on the "Not-seene Nimph" known as Avisa.

There are other points of contact between Eliot and "Henrie Willobie". We have noticed the anti-alien ten- dency of the *Ortho-epia Gallica* and how it was aimed at Frenchmen, Italians, Dutchmen, and others. "Willobie" also displays an interest in aliens by making several of Avisa's suitors foreigners. "Caveleiro" one is called, and this has a foreign sound. After "Caveleiro" comes "D. B. A French man". To him succeeds "Dydimvs Harco. Anglo-Germanus". Whilst that ardent young man "H. W." is described as "Henrico Willobego. Italo-Hispa-lensis".[1] There is thus a distinctly foreign atmosphere in *Willobie*, a sense of the presence of persons of varying nationalities, as there is also in the *Ortho-epia Gallica*.

It is significant, too, that when "H. W." and Avisa are conversing an Italian proverb is always appended to their speeches. As Dr Harrison notes,[2] no fewer than seven of these Italian mottoes are to be found in Florio's *Giardino di Ricreatione*, the proverb collection which his *Second Fruits* was designed to illustrate. This and other con- siderations had earlier led Mr Arthur Acheson[3] and the Countess de Chambrun[4] to search for further traces of Florio in *Willobie His Avisa*.

Clearly, then, there is what one might call a flavour of the Eliot-Florio situation in *Willobie His Avisa*. I am, moreover, much struck by the words with which Avisa

[1] "Henrico Willobego", the suitor, was apparently not the same individual as "Henrie Willobie" the author.
[2] *Willobie His Avisa, ed. cit.* p. 219.
[3] *Shakespeare's Last Years in London*, 1920, pp. 186-7.
[4] *Giovanni Florio*, pp. 114-21.

greets Caveleiro on his first appearance. Her speech of reply to his first speech begins thus:

> What now? what newes? new warres in hand?
> More trumpets blowne of fond conceites?[1]

Now Eliot's address to the professors of the French tongue in London which is the first of the two English prefaces to *Ortho-epia Gallica* and in which he challenged the alien teachers in the city opens with these words:

> *Messires*, what newes from Fraunce, can you tell? Still warres, warres.[2]

This preface, which had so much in common with the proscribed anti-alien libels of 1593, must have had a certain notoriety and I think that Avisa was thinking of its opening words when she greeted her first alien lover. The phrase also occurs elsewhere in the *Ortho-epia Gallica*, in the dialogue on "The Exchange".

> VVhat newes in Fraunce?
> None that I can tell, still vvarre, vvarre.[3]

It will be remembered that Eliot was a translator of French news-letters and so naturally an authority on news from France. "News" came into Harvey's mind in connection with Eliot, for after his quotation in *Pierces Supererogation* of the sentiments on "artist" and "villanist" which he attributed to Eliot he says:

> Something else was vttered the same time by the same Gentleman, aswell concerning the present state of France, which he termed the most vnchristian kingdome of the most christian kinge; as touching certaine other newes of I wott not what dependence.[4]

---

[1] *Willobie His Avisa, ed. cit.* p. 58.
[2] *Ortho-epia Gallica*, sig. A3: *Parlement of Pratlers*, p. 19.
[3] *Ortho-epia Gallica*, sig. *d*2: *Parlement of Pratlers*, p. 28.
[4] See Appendix I, pp. 204-5.

This suggests that Eliot was not only a purveyor of French news but also of some other kind of mysterious news or gossip.

Another scattered piece which I believe belongs to the *Willobie* puzzle lurks in one of Nashe's pamphlets. Into his *Have With You to Saffron Walden*, published in 1596, Nashe introduces someone who makes a speech praising his rival, Harvey. As Dr McKerrow points out,[1] this is obviously an imitation or parody of the way in which Harvey had quoted a speech in praise of Nashe in *Pierces Supererogation*. As we now know that that speech was meant to be by Eliot, it seems likely that when Nashe reminded his readers of it he also would be thinking of Eliot. The following is Nashe's parody of the Eliot speech:

[Harvey's style is commended by many persons.] Amongst the which number is a red-bearded thrid-bare Caualier, who (in my hearing) at an ordinarie, as he sat fumbling the dice after supper, fell into these tearmes (no talke before leading him to it): There is such a Booke of *Harueys* (meaning this his last Booke against mee), as I am a Souldiour and a Gentleman, I protest, I neuer met with the like contriued pile of pure English. O, it is deuine and most admirable, & so farre beyond all that euer he published heretofore, as day-light beyond candle-light, or tinsell or leafe-gold aboue arsedine; with a great many more excessiue praises he bestowed vpon it: which authentically I should haue beleeued, if, immediately vpon the nicke of it, I had not seene him shrug his shoulders, and talk of going to the *Bathe*, and after, like a true Pandar (so much the fitter to be one of *Gabriels* Patrons), grew in commending to yong gentlemen two or three of the most detested loathsom whores about *London*, for peereles beauteous Paragons & the pleasingest wenches in the world.[2]

"Caualier" suggests "Caveleiro", "ordinarie" suggests an inn or tavern, "dice" reminds one that the "Caveleiro"

---

[1] T. Nashe, *Works*, ed. R. B. McKerrow, IV, 322.

[2] *Ibid*. III, 41–2.

of *Willobie* is described as a dicer and gamester,[1] and so there are a good many reasons for supposing that Nashe was here connecting the speaker of the "villanists" versus "artists" speech in *Pierces Supererogation* with the *Willobie His Avisa* scandals, whatever they were. There appears to have been a second edition of *Willobie* about 1596, which is the year in which Nashe published the above speech.

It is my belief, therefore, that *Ortho-epia Gallica* ought to be studied in connection with *Willobie His Avisa*. Shakespeare is mentioned by name in *Willobie* and I would even go so far as to suggest that he may be hinted at in *Ortho-epia Gallica*. The "Ieronimo Pierruche" in Eliot's last dialogue, who was in love and engrossed in stringing together Petrarcan conceits to his mistress, was often seen to "counterfait Sisyphus, to play the Tantalus, to represent Titius Tragedie".[2] Was "Ieronimo Pierruche" then an actor? Shakespeare was acting in *Titus Andronicus* in 1592, which appears to be the year in which Eliot composed his dialogues.

*   *   *   *

We have now collected some pieces in the sequence which leads up to *Love's Labour's Lost* as its *finale*, and the foregoing arguments will perhaps become clearer if we now set out the pieces one by one in the right order. The whole sequence is concerned, roughly speaking, with a controversy concerning the rival merits of study and experience with Raleigh's friends and poets supporting the former and Essex's and Southampton's friends and poets supporting the latter. The former are the "artists", the latter the "villanists", and under these headings we shall classify the pieces for convenience sake. The terms are, however, only approximations to the two conflicting points

---

[1] Eliot's "pratlers" go to a dicing house, in brazen contradiction to Florio's speakers who had reprobated such places. *Ortho-epia Gallica*, sigs. *h* 1 v., *h* 2: *Parlement of Pratlers*, pp. 46–7.

[2] See p. 117.

of view, and Shakespeare is only labelled as a "villanist" here to show very roughly on which side of the dividing line his position lay. We shall attempt to examine his real attitude to the problem in the last chapter. No party label can cover his subtlety and profundity, and yet he did to some extent take a side in this controversy.

1593.	John Eliot's *Ortho-epia Gallica*.	"Villanist."
1593.	The "Eliot" speech in Gabriel Harvey's *Pierces Supererogation*.	"Villanist."
1594.	George Chapman's *Shadow of Night*.	"Artist."
1594.	*Willobie His Avisa*.	"Artist."
1594–5.	*Gesta Grayorum*.	"Villanist."
?	The Earl of Northumberland's essay.	"Artist."
?	*Love's Labour's Lost*.	"Villanist."

I believe that light may be thrown, not only on *Love's Labour's Lost*, but on Shakespeare's early career in general if these are all studied in connection with one another.

CHAPTER IX

The Date of *Love's Labour's Lost*

The task of attempting to date this play from external evidence is complicated by the question of revision. Was it written at one time in the form in which it was printed in the Quarto or was there an early version which was later revised and augmented and was the Quarto printed from this revised manuscript incorporating the first draft? Those who are best qualified to judge are not unanimous in their opinion. Professor Dover Wilson is in favour of revision and believes that he can detect which are the earlier and which the later parts of the play. Sir Edmund Chambers does not accept the revisionist view and thinks that the play was written more or less as we have it at one time. I therefore propose to review the evidence for dating under two heads.

I. ASSUMING NON-REVISION

If unrevised, the play is clearly later than the Gray's Inn Revels of 1594–5. I also think that one must allow for some little lapse of time after the revels during which the Earl of Northumberland's reactions developed and became apparent to Shakespeare, either through his having read the essay or having heard about the kind of line which the earl was taking. The play was, therefore, probably written some time during 1595 when the revels and Northumberland's reply to them were both recent history. It was no doubt first performed at a private house, perhaps the Earl of Southampton's, before an audience largely composed of ladies and gentlemen who had been present at the revels. It would thus be one of the causes contributing to the working up of ill-feeling between Northumberland and Southampton who were openly quarrelling late in 1596 and early in 1597.

It might, however, be argued that the play was written whilst the Northumberland-Southampton quarrel was going on, that is late in 1596 or early in 1597. This would agree with Mr Rupert Taylor who dates it in 1596 for quite a different reason, because he believes that he can detect in it echoes of Nashe's *Have With You to Saffron Walden* (1596).[1] Most of Mr Taylor's parallels between *Love's Labour's Lost* and *Have With You* are rather vague but some are certainly significant. I believe, however, that the explanation of these is, not that Shakespeare was borrowing from Nashe as Mr Taylor thinks, but that Nashe was borrowing from Shakespeare and was applying to Harvey some of the expressions which he had heard Holofernes and Armado use on the stage. Nashe must have taken a great interest in *Love's Labour's Lost* and would be very likely to allude to it in his *Have With You*, which also contains a parody of the Eliot speech in *Pierces Supererogation*.[2]

My conclusion therefore is that, if unrevised, the date of the play is 1595. This is the date assigned to *Love's Labour's Lost* by Sir Edmund Chambers.

II. ASSUMING REVISION

I do not think that any first draft, however meagre, can have been earlier than *Ortho-epia Gallica* and *Pierces Supererogation* in 1593. That is the year chosen by Professor Dover Wilson for his first version. He believes that Shakespeare saw Chapman's *Shadow of Night* (1594) in manuscript and that the dedication of that poem is a reply

---

[1] *The Date of Love's Labour's Lost*, pp. 34–51, 91–112.
[2] See pp. 166–7.

to the first draft of *Love's Labour's Lost*.[1] A revisionist might, I think, argue that a first draft was written in 1593 when *Ortho-epia Gallica* was very fresh and when Shakespeare was viewing current controversies from a rather similar angle to the Eliot speech in *Pierces Supererogation*. Chapman's dedication would then be a reply to both the early *Love's Labour's Lost* and to the Eliot speech. Such a first draft could have contained the eyes-stars, Petrarch-Pythagoras antithesis in some form, for the Bruno-Sidney-"Stella" side of that situation was already in existence in 1593. The revision and augmentation would come in 1595 when the entry of the Earl and Countess of Northumberland into the dispute and the Gray's Inn Revels would have made a play against the "School of Night", brought up to date, highly palatable to a select audience consisting largely of the Essex faction.

My own feeling, for what that is worth, is against any drastic revision. The play strikes me as having been reeled off all in one piece for a given situation, such as the one which existed in 1595. But the original manuscript may have been somewhat "revised" in the interests of safety before being handed to the printer. It was one thing to make political and personal allusions at a private performance amongst powerful friends, but it would be quite another, and much more dangerous, matter to print them in too clear a form.

The same considerations apply to the court performance. According to the title-page of the 1598 Quarto the play was performed at court "this last Christmas" which appears to mean Christmas 1597. This is the first performance for which there is definite evidence. It seems to me probable that there may have been slight differences between the play as originally written for a performance at (perhaps) Southampton's house in 1595 and the play as

[1] *Love's Labour's Lost* in the Cambridge *New Shakespeare*, pp. 126–7.

performed at court at Christmas 1597. For the latter performance the anti-alien and anti-Florio allusions would be toned down or entirely muted whilst the vindication of the star-like ladies would become a compliment from Essex to Elizabeth and to the ladies of her court. The anti-Raleigh and anti-Northumberland allusions would be safe at court for Raleigh was out of favour and Elizabeth did not approve of hermit-like noblemen[1] who did not keep up a proper state and refused to transact her business.[2]

In 1605 the play was revived and was acted at Southampton's house to amuse Queen Anne. Florio was by then secretary and reader in Italian to the Queen. One may note, too, that Lady Rich and her sister were popular with Anne and that this year was to see the ruin of the Earl of Northumberland over the Gunpowder Plot. He was sent to join his friend Raleigh in the Tower, where, under the guidance of Hariot and others, they turned their compulsory retirement from the sweet world into an opportunity for the deep search for knowledge.

[1] Something of this kind is possibly the trend of the masque by Bacon which Essex presented to the Queen in 1595. See pp. 157–8, note 1.

[2] In July 1596, Northumberland refused to undertake an embassy into France. (*Salisbury Papers*, VI, pp. 260–1.) This might be reflected upon in the rather pointed words in which Boyet undertakes to be the bearer of a message from the Princess to Navarre:

"Proud of employment, willingly I go." (II. i. 35.)

I do not think, however, that a small point of this kind is sufficient to date the composition of the play in 1596 when the Gray's Inn Revels atmosphere of it points so strongly to 1595. It is more likely to have been put in later to bring the court performance up to date.

CHAPTER X

The Characters of *Love's Labour's Lost* and Italian Comedy

Do the four young men of *Love's Labour's Lost* represent the Essex group, or are they Raleigh's "artists"? As in the case of the comic characters, "original"-seeking must be avoided. Touches of Raleigh and of Northumberland, and perhaps of Carey and of Strange (who died in 1594) are possibly to be detected in Navarre and his three friends. But so also are touches of Essex[1] and of his two young companions Southampton and Rutland (both of whom were Florio's pupils). Berowne is perhaps a kind of combination of Essex and Bruno, pondering in his divided mind the two

---

[1] Mr Hoyt H. Hudson (in the article referred to on p. 107, note 1) mentions a book called *Deuoreux. Vertues teares for the losse of...King Henry...and the vntimely death, of...Walter Deuoreux*, 1597. This is a translation by Gervase Markham of a French elegy on the death of Essex's brother whose memory is coupled with that of King Henry III of France. Here is an example of a "French news" name being associated with that of a member of the Devereux family. Moreover, Markham dedicates his translation to the Countess of Northumberland and to Lady Rich by the influence of whose gracious eyes he hopes that "the worst of my penns earthines doubtlesse shall be stellified". He also addresses stanzas to the two sisters in which he says

"For who that speakes, speakes not with double fire
If but one thought of them glaunce in his song."
(Cp. *L.L.L.* IV. iii. 328.)

And in another line he addresses Lady Rich as "thou rich, *Rich*, richest". (Cp. *L.L.L.* V. ii. 158–9.) I have not been able to see a copy of this book but it sounds as though it might provide additional confirmation of some of my arguments. Gervase Markham has been suggested as possibly the author of *A Health to the Gentlemanly Profession of Serving-Men*, 1598 (Shakespeare Association Facsimiles, No. 3), in which a joke from *Love's Labour's Lost* is quoted.

sides of the controversy. And it is also suggestive to think here of the contrasting ways in which Bacon and Shakespeare used "light" imagery.

As to the four ladies, the genius of the Devereux sisters probably inspired some of their wit and gaiety, but it would be going much too far to say that Rosaline (who, unlike Lady Rich, has black hair as well as black eyes) *is* one of them, or that the Princess with her fondness for a hundred thousand crowns *is* the other. Moreover, there were other ladies in the Essex group who could be connected in one way or another with Sidney or with "Stella". The wife of Essex was Sidney's widow and to her Spenser dedicated in 1595 his *Astrophel* in praise of her first husband. The wife of Rutland was Sidney's daughter (and to her and Lady Rich together Florio dedicated a part of his *Montaigne*). Southampton eventually married Elizabeth Vernon who was Lady Rich's cousin.

There was yet another living lady famous for her connection with Sidney, his sister the Countess of Pembroke for whom the *Arcadia* was written and to whose sons Shakespeare's plays were long afterwards dedicated. Her annoyance at the clandestine publication of her brother's *Astrophel and Stella* in 1591 and at Fulke Greville's edition of his *Arcadia* in 1590 was one of the reasons why Sidney's work was so "topical" in this decade. Nashe and Samuel Daniel were connected with the unauthorised *Astrophel and Stella* and Florio was probably connected with the unauthorised *Arcadia*. They were rebuked for their meddling by the Pembroke agent and secretary, Hugh Sanford, and out of this arose a quarrel between Sanford, Florio and Nashe in the course of which the meek Daniel came in for some nasty knocks and had his sonnets criticised by Sanford. Some of this may come into the play, and Dr G. B. Harrison is, I think, right in drawing attention to Daniel in connection with *Love's Labour's Lost*.[1]

[1] G. B. Harrison, *An Elizabethan Journal*, 1928, p. 399.

Daniel was tutor to the Pembroke son and heir and so might claim some right of way into the schoolmaster class of "originals". But all this Pembroke side of the situation is, as yet, so obscure that it seems unsafe to theorise concerning Shakespeare's attitude to it. One can see, however, that Nashe and Florio might enter the play as Sidney's editors as well as through other doors.

In the main plot, then, are reflected certain exalted personages. In the sub-plot are shadows of their numerous literary dependants and hangers-on, Chapman, Hariot, Harvey, Nashe, Florio and the foreign teachers, Eliot, Daniel, Antonio Perez (a queer Spaniard who wrote queer letters, rather like Armado's, some of them to Lady Rich)[1] and perhaps others. Moreover, the eccentricities of the more unpopular of the exalted personages—Raleigh and Northumberland—may also be hinted at in the fantastics of the sub-plot.

Yet not one of these people can be picked out as being definitely the "original" of any one character; firstly, because Shakespeare was too creative to use his human material so crudely; secondly, because he was cautious in avoiding trouble with the authorities, and thirdly, because he probably took the rough outline of the plot and the characters ready made from some source which has not yet been determined.

*　　　*　　　*　　　*

The possibility of an Italianate origin for the whole plot of *Love's Labour's Lost* might, I think, be further explored. The parallel arrangement of the four men and the four women, the disguise scene in which the pairs change partners for a while, these things seem full of the atmosphere of Italian comedy, as well as the faintly "mask-like" nature of Holofernes the pedant, Armado the braggart, Boyet

[1] Martin Hume, *Spanish Influence on English Literature*, 1905, pp. 258–74.

who is called a "zany" and is a go-between, Costard the rustic, Jaquenetta the serving-wench who pairs with the braggart. Amongst the English plays in which Miss Lea thinks that she can detect the influence of an Italian scenario is *The Wit of a Woman*.[1] Here the lovers are in four pairs; the men disguise themselves as teachers and tutors in order to get into contact with the girls. They set up their teaching "signs". They "discover their intentions in dialogues full of facetious equivocation" and "the scene ends with a dance". There is a captain who falls in love with a wench called Gianetta and a doctor who quotes Latin tags. Compare this with the four pairs in *Love's Labour's Lost*, the equivocating dialogue when the men woo the women in Russian disguise and they all take part in a dance, the braggart Armado who loves a wench called Jaquenetta, the pedant Holofernes who quotes tags of Latin, and the conclusion seems obvious that if *The Wit of a Woman* is based on an Italian scenario, then so is *Love's Labour's Lost*. Again, take another play in which Miss Lea sees Italian influence, Haughton's *Englishmen for My Money*. Here there are three pairs, the girls being engaged at the start in studying "philosophy" which they renounce for love. A comparison might be drawn between this and the men in *Love's Labour's Lost* who renounce philosophy for love and we have elsewhere suggested that Haughton's play also contains traces of Eliot's attack on the aliens. If Haughton's anti-alien play has an Italianate origin, then so might Shakespeare's.

The four pairs of men and women and some of the intrigue in *Love's Labour's Lost* are thus perhaps a rough pattern derived from some Italian scenario, just as the *commedia dell' arte* types of the pedant and the braggart were rough sketches for Holofernes and Armado. I think that the "French-news" names and the scraps of French history were not in the original play or plot which Shake-

[1] *Italian Popular Comedy*, II, 413–15.

speare used but were his additions to it.¹ The four men, perhaps, originally had Italian names. Their French names were a part of their "topicality", introduced by Shakespeare, and that topicality was not only of a public character, connected with current events abroad, but had also a more private significance, associated with Essex, Southampton and their friends.

This attempt to connect *Love's Labour's Lost* with some hypothetical Italian plot may sound somewhat unconvincing and of course it is not proven. But curiously enough, once again this is a subject about which Eliot has something to say, for the author of *Ortho-epia Gallica* was evidently very familiar with the *commedia dell' arte* and must have been present at performances given by travelling Italian comedians. This can be proved as follows.

In Eliot's dialogue called "The Bragger" a person of the name of "seignior Crocodill" (spelt "Cocodrill" in the address to the readers²) boasts mightily of his strength and of his prowess in arms, interlarding his speech with strange oaths and wildly exaggerated expressions. Nevertheless, when the enemies appear on the scene crying "Sassassa, kill, kill", the boastful Crocodill turns out to be a coward and yields to them without striking a blow, muttering miserably that he is "affeard to die".³ The whole vivid, noisy dialogue strikes one as being a transcript from a stage-scene, as indeed it undoubtedly is.

Among the well-known stage types or masks round which the Italian comedians built up their improvised popular comedy, or *commedia dell' arte*, was the boastful captain who was braver in words than in deeds. None of the masks of Italian comedy was better known than this bragging, professional soldier. The "captain" was known

---

¹ Professor Dover Wilson thinks, however, that Shakespeare used some "French comedy". Cambridge *New Shakespeare*, L.L.L. p. 130.

² See p. 163.

³ *Ortho-epia Gallica*, sigs. r4–t1: *Parlement of Pratlers*, pp. 98–102.

by different names when interpreted by different actors. The noted Francesco Andreini of the "Gelosi" troupe made him famous under the name of "Capitano Spavento del Vall' Inferno"; but in the hands of Fabrizio de Fornaris, of the "Confidenti" he was known as "Captain Cocodrillo". Professor Allardyce Nicoll has pointed out that Eliot's "seigneur Cocodrill" is undoubtedly the same as the Capitan Cocodrillo of Italian comedy and that the "bragger" dialogue "reproduces Eliot's memory of the words which he must have heard uttered upon the stage by Fabrizio de Fornaris".[1] Whether Eliot had seen the Italian comedians during his travels in France and Italy or on one of their visits to England it is impossible to say, but the fact remains that he *had* seen them, that they had made some considerable impression upon his imagination and memory, and that by introducing the bragging "capitano" into one of his dialogues he carried the modern-language dialogue almost to the boards of the stage.

Another hint of Eliot's familiarity with Italian comedy is the fact that the picture in the painter's shop—which we thought might be meant as a portrait of Florio—is called "an Italian Harlekin".[2] Possibly, too, the "doctor" or "pedant" of Italian comedy is hinted at in the following remark in Eliot's concluding dialogue:

I heare now a thing worthy of a poets vaine.

What then? didst thou looke for something smelling of a philosophers braine? Seeke that of these new *magistri inertes* of the vniuersitie. Many of them are philosophers in their gownes, and by their wits countrie clownes.

Say then that they are doctors of Valentia, vvith long gownes and little *scientia*.[3]

[1] Allardyce Nicoll, *Masks, Mimes, and Miracles*, 1931, pp. 250, 309. See also K. M. Lea, *Italian Popular Comedy*, 1934, I, 48, note 2; II, 397.

[2] See p. 44.

[3] *Ortho-epia Gallica*, sig. t4: *Parlement of Pratlers*, p. 105.

However, this touch is not quite original, being a development of a sneer by Vives at Parisian doctors.

I believe that there is an echo of Eliot's "Cocodrill" in the masque of the Nine Worthies in *Love's Labour's Lost*. Critics have been much exercised in mind because Shakespeare's worthies are not the conventional choice.[1] Hector, Alexander and Judas Maccabæus were, it is true, to be found among the usually selected nine, but not Pompey and Hercules. Moreover, the introduction of Hercules "in minority"[2] and strangling a snake is unusual, though natural enough in the context in view of the extreme youth of Moth who was to take the part. I would here point out that amongst the brags of "seigneur Cocodrill", quoted by Eliot, occurs the following:

Truly Hercules is nothing to you, vvho being in the cradle, kild the two Serpents: for the said Serpents vvere verie litle and vveake things.[3]

Might not this have given Shakespeare the idea for Hercules in minority strangling the serpent? It is noteworthy too, that immediately after the mention of Hercules, "seigneur Cocodrill" boasts that he could most easily vanquish "Hector that Troian Lad" or "Alexander, the great drunkard of Greece". Later on Pompey is also mentioned, with other Roman notables. The braggart captain thus names nearly all (though not Joshua and Judas Maccabæus) the "worthies" introduced by Shakespeare into the masque acted by his Italianate characters, "the pedant, the braggart, the hedge-priest, the fool, and the boy", and sketches one of them in the same unusual attitude in which Shakespeare presents him. This seems to me to strengthen, not only the connection between *Ortho-epia Gallica* and *Love's*

---

[1] The controversy is summarised by J. H. Roberts in "The Nine Worthies", *Modern Philology*, 1921–2, XIX, 297–305.

[2] v. ii. 588.

[3] *Ortho-epia Gallica*, sig. s2: *Parlement of Pratlers*, p. 100.

Labour's Lost which has been established on other counts, but the connection between *Love's Labour's Lost* and the *commedia dell' arte*. Eliot could have helped Shakespeare to an Italian plot, as well as to "French news" and history.

Certain other jokes in this play may have behind them, as well as their personal and topical satire, some more general memory of the patter of the Italian comedians. Miss Lea notes that the doctor used words like "certifica-bilitudinitissimamient"[1] which may be compared with Costard's "honorificabilitudinitatibus". She also suggests that the lists of great men who have been in love with which Moth comforts Armado are reminiscent of Andreini's *Bravure*.[2] A parody of a sonnet was a frequent diversion with the Italian comedians, which is to be noted in connection with the efforts of Holofernes in this direction, whilst the "serious" mask of the "inamorato" indulged in real sonnet-making, varied by anti-Petrarchistic abuse when his affairs were not going well. The sonnet-writing and discussions on love in *Love's Labour's Lost* are thus in the tradition of the Italian stage.[3]

These and other points suggest to me that Shakespeare worked from some rough Italianate outline[4] for the plot as well as for some of the characterisation in this play, and this must be remembered and allowed for in any attempt to assess its topical importance. But he probably deliberately chose a plot which suited the situation and the people which he had in mind.

[1] K. M. Lea, *op. cit.* I, 39.   [2] *Ibid.* II, 398.

[3] The importance now attached to the memory of Sidney and of Sidney's works in *Love's Labour's Lost* rather strengthens the suggestion that the Italianate pedant, Rombus, in Sidney's masque *The Lady of May*, might have given points to Holofernes. See Introduction, p. 17.

[4] This might, of course, have been some English play imitated from the Italians. There must have been many "casts of Italian devices" now lost, like those of Stephen Gosson.

As an example of how he combined his hits at a living "original" with his ready-made Italian pattern one may take the case of Florio. To present Florio with a more or less "right" Italian comedy,[1] such as he was always bemoaning the lack of in England, in which the Pedant bore a strong resemblance to himself would have been a peculiarly subtle form of satire. Nothing would have annoyed Florio more than to be called a pedant, for this was just what he thought he was not. One of his pedantic affectations was the affectation of not being a pedant. He was well up in all the latest modern ideas. He had been the friend of Bruno who despised the old-fashioned type of Aristotelian and grammarian more than he despised anyone, and that is saying a great deal for Bruno was a scornful person. Florio with his open, alert mind, his modern outlook, his fashionable style in speaking and writing, his pleasingly facetious attitude to polite pleasures, was quite certain that *he* was not a pedant. The subtle point of Shakespeare's satire was that the new learning might have its pedants as well as the old, that members of the "School of Night" who had left the schoolmen's vulgar, trodden paths might be quite as absurd in their way as the old-fashioned Aristotelian race of pedants whom they despised. How the implication rankled with Florio is shown by the way in which he passed it on to Sanford in his dictionary preface. Sanford is therein called a "reading grammarian-pedante".[2] Curiously enough, too, when he wrote that preface he must recently have been translating Montaigne's essay "Of pedantisme", for he uses a metaphor from it concerning seeds carried in the beaks of birds and coins passed from hand to hand.[3] Montaigne uses these figures in the essay on pedantry to illustrate how the learning of the pedant is a thing external to himself which he passes on to

---

[1] *Love's Labour's Lost* is, however, not quite "right" from Florio's point of view because kings and clowns are mingled in it.
[2] *John Florio*, p. 338. [3] *Ibid.* pp. 213–14.

others, and makes a great show of, but which he has not himself properly assimilated, experienced or understood. So pedantic learning "passeth from hand to hand, to this end only, thereby to make a glorious shew". With what zest and interest contemporaries who knew Florio must have read this chapter in his great translation when it appeared, and with what amusement they must have noted the sentence with which it opens: "I have in my youth oftentimes beene vexed, to see a Pedant brought in, in most of Italian comedies, for a vice or sport-maker, and the nicke-name of *Magister* to be of no better signification amongst us."

CHAPTER XI

Shakespeare—Some Deductions

Some of the material which has been used as the basis of this study has hitherto either partially or entirely escaped the serious attention of Shakespearean experts. If I have proved a connection between *Love's Labour's Lost* and these various books and documents, they must become a small addition to the sources whence our knowledge of Shakespeare's environment is derived. What have we learnt about Shakespeare himself during our attempts to relate this play to its surroundings?

The first and perhaps the most important to notice is that if there is a kind of *apologia* for Essex's two sisters in *Love's Labour's Lost* this must very considerably strengthen the Southampton school of thought in regard to Shakespeare. Southampton admired Essex's brilliant sisters as much as he admired Essex himself. He took the Countess of Northumberland's part against her husband; he was antagonistic to the Raleigh group and their speculations. The attitude of Shakespeare as interpreted in this book was thus exactly suited to the earl's outlook, and if that interpretation is accepted it should go far towards justifying those who have always placed Shakespeare on terms of intimacy with Southampton during these years.

There are a large number of close correspondences in thought and language between *Love's Labour's Lost* and Shakespeare's sonnets. That has always been recognised, and the corollary to it is that if some part of the play's secret is now revealed this should be of use to students of the sonnets. We have seen that the play is full of the influence of Sidney. No one who lived within the Southampton *ambience* which was crowded with Sidney's relations and friends could help being constantly reminded of him. No one who read at all, even if only to curtail a tedious hour, could miss seeing copies of the authorised and unauthorised editions of *Astrophel and Stella* and of the *Arcadia* which succeeded one another from 1590 onwards, or could avoid hearing of the controversies which they aroused. One could not even try to learn a little French or Italian without being reminded of these. The argument between "artists" and "villanists", between Raleigh's friends and Essex's friends, turned upon the sonnet-writing fashion as one of its pivots. To love or not to love, to write arcadian "platts" to ladies or not to write them—that was the question in the air, and it was given point and poignancy by the living presence of the original "Stella" herself. A writer of sugared sonnets during these years must surely have been influenced by these currents and cross-currents. I suggest, in particular, that in view of the prominence which Florio gave to the philosophical discussion between Bruno and Sidney, the whole question of Bruno's influence in the sonnets might be re-examined.

The candidature of Chapman for the position of the "rival poet" has also, I think, been somewhat strengthened. Not only his *Shadow of Night* but also his *Coronet for his Mistress Philosophy* (1595) seem to have certain affinities with the Earl of Northumberland's essay and if I have proved that *Love's Labour's Lost* was a contradiction of that essay, or at least of the attitude to which it gives expression, it follows that the play was also a contradiction of Chapman and that there was a kind of argument or rivalry between Shakespeare and Chapman during these years.

Another personage who has been prominent in the labyrinth of *Love's Labour's Lost* is the strange individual who did not love the foreign language teachers. It seems to me that the fact that John Eliot has turned up, not merely once but many times, as the argument has twisted hither and thither is an indication that he was fairly close to Shakespeare at this time. Who mocked the textbooks of the manual writers with the same kind of Rabelaisian laughter as is to be heard in the play? Who expressed to Harvey views on "artists" and "villanists" not unlike those in the play? Whom does Chapman seem to be classing with Shakespeare in his attack on those who pretend to pierce to the heart of truth by their natural wits alone? Who knew a poet who had represented "Titius Tragedie"? Who suggested that a satirical comedy might be written on the aliens and who muttered mysteriously about Aristophanes and the songs of birds? Of whom might Avisa be thinking when she mentions news of wars? Why does the Bastard in *King John* talk about question and answer in an "absey" book and determine to cultivate a "mounting spirit", and who is in the mind of Sir Toby Belch's creator when he associates learning the tongues with hair curled by Nature or by Art? Finally, why are the words inserted in the Folio text at the very end of *Love's Labour's Lost* practically the same as the words at the end of Eliot's last dialogue?[1]

I do not know how all this will strike the reader. It strikes me as being circumstantial evidence which seems to point towards John Eliot as having been one of Shakespeare's associates in the Southampton circle. It must be carefully emphasised that there is as yet no documentary evidence to connect Eliot with that circle (unless one can count the fact that he dedicated a book to Essex in 1591).[2] But I think that it would not be an over-statement of the

---

[1] "You that way: we this way." (*L.L.L.*, Folio text only.) "Lets go this vvay: lets go that vvay. Along, along." (*Ortho-epia Gallica*, sig. *y*3: *Parlement of Pratlers*, p. 114.) Might this suggest that the allusions to Eliot and the foreigners were more obvious in the acted version than in the printed version of the play?

[2] *John Florio*, p. 177.

case to say that Eliot's *Ortho-epia Gallica* has now been proved to be a book which was known to Shakespeare and that, further, a certain friendship or *camaraderie* between Eliot and Shakespeare during the earlier fifteen-nineties, although not perhaps absolutely proven, is a hypothesis which certainly fits in very neatly and conveniently with many of the known facts of the situation. Moreover, I think it is a hypothesis which might be worth working. The assumption of some connection between Eliot and Shakespeare would be an entirely new point from which to start the exploration of that unknown ground, Shakespeare's career before 1592. And when one starts to think along these lines one is struck by several rather curious coincidences.

In the first place, Eliot tells us that he was a native of Warwickshire:[1] we all know well enough that this was Shakespeare's county. Secondly, he was roughly the contemporary in age of the dramatist, being about two years older.[2] Thirdly, he was a schoolmaster or teacher of sorts: scholarship has been tending more and more in recent years towards the rehabilitation of Aubrey's statement that Shakespeare started life as a schoolmaster in the country.[3] Fourthly, I strongly suspect Eliot of having been a Catholic,[4] though this is not absolutely proven: the recusancy of Shakespeare's father seems to be fairly well established and a good many scholars are now of the opinion that Shakespeare's own sympathies inclined to the old religion. Fifthly, Eliot knew Robert Greene[5] who is the first person to mention (in 1592) Shakespeare's presence in London. Eliot and Shakespeare thus certainly had in common age, county, and some acquaintance with Robert Greene, and possibly began life in the same profession and with the

---

[1] *John Florio*, p. 174. [2] *Ibid., loc. cit.*
[3] See J. S. Smart, *Shakespeare Truth and Tradition*; Peter Alexander, *Shakespeare's Henry VI and Richard III.*
[4] *John Florio*, p. 187. [5] *Ibid.* pp. 174-5.

same (again "possibly") religious convictions. All this is, of course, uncertain and vague in itself, but when taken in conjunction with the way in which Eliot seems to keep cropping up in the territory immediately surrounding *Love's Labour's Lost* it is not without significance.

Upon these foundations, which I acknowledge to be, as yet, somewhat insecure, I venture to build the following theory.

Let us suppose that Shakespeare did indeed begin life as a schoolmaster, as Beeston told Aubrey, but as a Catholic schoolmaster. That is to say, that he taught, not in some country grammar-school, but in some secret Catholic school, of the type of the one kept by Swithin Wells at Monkton Farleigh, or was tutor in the house of some Catholic nobleman. The latter suggestion has already been put forward by Professor Dover Wilson who hints that Shakespeare might have first come into contact with the Catholic Earl of Southampton in the capacity of a tutor[1]— an idea which would fit in remarkably well with certain aspects of the present study. For it will be remembered that there was a schism in the Southampton household between the old Catholic friends of the family and the influence of Burleigh, the Protestant guardian, and that Florio was probably put into the position of language tutor to the earl by Burleigh after the destruction of the Catholic Swithin Wells. Now if Shakespeare and Eliot were both teachers or tutors in attendance on Southampton at some time or another and in sympathy with the Catholic party in his household, would not the attack on Florio and the Protestant aliens by Eliot in *Ortho-epia Gallica* and by

[1] *The Essential Shakespeare*, p. 64. Professor Dover Wilson goes on to note that "the earl had one tutor in residence with him, John Florio, the translator of Montaigne, whose influence upon Shakespeare has been remarked by many critics; and if the dramatist acted as Florio's colleague for some months, his interest in the great French humanist would be explained".

Shakespeare in *Love's Labour's Lost* at once admit of an explanation as expressions—extremely indirect and round-about expressions, of course—of the young earl's annoyance and disgust at his guardian's efforts to dragoon him into religious conformity through his education? Of course, this is nothing but a guess and must remain so unless documentary evidence in support of it comes to light. But I do suggest to record searchers whose ambition it is to find out something about Shakespeare before 1592 that the secret Catholic schools, the Catholic friends and dependents of Southampton's father, and all traces of John Eliot might be worth their attention.

In the meantime the dialogues of Eliot and Florio await the further attention of experts. Both Florio and Eliot use second-hand material constantly, but they may quite often be twisting it to some local theme. Their manuals should be combed for hints. And if it should be objected that these are after all only modern-language textbooks and, as such, not likely to be very informative concerning the circles for which they were written, one might reply with a short history of the language-dialogue as an educational power, which would run somewhat as follows.

The modern language-dialogue was the child of the Latin "colloquy", as has already been said. These colloquies were written primarily to instruct children in the art of Latin speaking and were widely used in England.[1] In the first half of the sixteenth century the colloquies of Vives and Erasmus were the most popular. The strict moral tone of Vives made him agreeable to the educationalists who were anxious to counteract the influences of pagan literature. Erasmus's dialogues were very much read outside as well as inside schools. Their tone of dissatisfaction with the abuses in the Church made them acceptable to the Reformation temper, and their up-to-date and amusing

[1] See Foster Watson, *English Grammar Schools to 1660*, 1908, pp. 325–48.

treatment of questions of the hour caused them to be much in demand. In the case of the *Colloquia* of Erasmus we see a book, ostensibly designed as an aid to Latin speaking and the improvement of Latin style, taking upon itself functions which we should to-day associate with leading articles in newspapers or political weeklies.

In the latter half of the sixteenth century in England the dialogues of Erasmus and Vives were rivalled and surpassed in popularity, though not superseded, by those of Sébastien Castellion and of Corderius (Mathurin Cordier). The English Reformation temper had advanced during the century from an Erasmian discontent to open secession and the change is reflected in the colloquies. Castellion and Corderius teach in their dialogues a definitely Protestant and anti-Catholic point of view and for this reason they were used in schools throughout Protestant Europe. Corderius was particularly popular in England and was to be found lurking in out-of-the-way schools right up to the early nineteenth century. In spite of his didactic and moralising tendencies his dialogues are interesting and lively transcripts from life.

When the Latin colloquy finally died out of use and was no more seen in schools, or out of them, the larger political and satirical importance which it had once held was forgotten also, until Professor Foster Watson pointed this out. "The Colloquy began in the time of the Renascence", he says, "by being a school method of teaching Latin on the model of Terence and Cicero, but it developed into a method of bringing the vital problems of the age into the school-room, in a form calculated to be suitable to the child. It became the most living, developing method of bringing the young pupil into early touch with the intellectual and spiritual atmosphere of the times. The classical authors were fixed, and were un-Christian. The Colloquy may thus be represented as a counter-balance. In the seventeenth century culture, theology was in the schools

at least what science is to-day and represented the pro-
gressive element in the school curriculum, largely through
the Colloquy. The changes of thought in the religious
world can be traced in large characters in the *Colloquies*,
as they pass from the pages of Mosellanus to those of
Erasmus, from Erasmus to Vives, from Vives to Castellion
and Corderius. The Colloquy, in a word, in its later
development was a means of bringing the school into relation with life."[1]

One may add that with Erasmus the colloquy came out
of the school and addressed itself to adult readers interested
in current affairs. His colloquy on love and marriage is a
reminder of the feminist movement among contemporary
humanists.[2] Another on "The Alchemist" ridicules the
craze for alchemy. Erasmus used his own experiences and
those of his friends as illustration and argument. He introduced the names of his pupils into the dialogues.[3] He
attacked the "sophistical riddles, vain babbling, sycophancy,
arrogance, virulence, sardonic humor, thrasonical boasting,
and self-love" of a certain "N" who is thought to be
Edward Lee with whom he had a quarrel. In some
dialogues he is probably describing his own love-experiences
and in his bitterness against the forcing of young people
to take monastic vows was doubtless thinking of the way
in which he had himself been tricked into the monastery.
"The Discontented Wife" tells various stories of married
life which seem to have been derived from the experiences
of Erasmus's friends. The first anecdote was proved by the
late Dr Percy Allen to depict a scene from the married
life of Sir Thomas More, and another story about astrology

[1] Foster Watson, *op. cit.* p. 346.

[2] This and other points concerning the topical side of Erasmus's
dialogues are taken from *A Key to the Colloquies of Erasmus*, by
Preserved Smith. Harvard Theological Studies, 1927, XIII.

[3] This was a usual practise with the writers of colloquies. See
J. Le Coultre, *Maturin Cordier et les origines de la pédagogie protestante
dans les pays de langue française*, 1926, p. 370.

seems also to be connected with More. The dialogues of
Erasmus must therefore have had a very particular interest
within his own circle, in addition to their larger appeal.
Undoubtedly he represents the high-water mark of the
Latin colloquy as satire and as a social document.

In its own rather smaller and less noticeable way the
modern-language dialogue was the heir to all these things.
We have seen how the themes of the modern-language
dialogues were often imitated from the Latin dialogues.
But the resemblance between these two classes of book
goes deeper than a mere borrowing of themes. Into some
of the modern-language dialogues the larger traditions of
the Latin colloquy, as outlined above, are seen to enter.
For example, Florio's *First Fruits* presents a somewhat
Puritanical theology and morality. It seems to have been
designed to provide Italian culture in a form which would
be palatable to left-wing adherents of the Elizabethan
settlement, such as Lord Burleigh.[1] In this way it is allied
to the Latin colloquy of "Protestant" tone. Again the
humour, the satire, the use of personal experience in Eliot's
Ortho-epia Gallica bring it into line, however distantly,
with the colloquies of Erasmus. Eliot mentions Erasmus
by name.[2] His story of the man who tried on shoes at the
shoemaker's and then ran away with them on his feet without paying for them can be paralleled in Erasmus's dialogues. Some of the jokes about mixing water and wine,
the adulteration of beer, and so on, also seem at times

[1] See *John Florio*, pp. 36, 52–3.
[2] Erasmus, he says, doubted not but that Cicero might be saved
for "he hath spoken so diuinely of God". *Ortho-epia Gallica*, sig. G 2.
A possible link between Erasmus and *Love's Labour's Lost* is suggested by Mr James Hutton who points out (*Modern Language Notes*,
June 1931, XLVI, 392–5) that Costard's word "honorificabilitudinitatibus" is used in Erasmus's *Adagia*, where it is associated with an
unknown person called "Hermes". (If this Hermes could be connected in any way with Hermes Trismegistus, it might account for
the appearance of this word in an anti-"artist" comedy.)

reminiscent of Erasmus's brand of humour. The *Ortho-epia Gallica* is a much slighter performance in every way than the famous dialogues of the great Dutch scholar and its author, though an extremely amusing fellow, was a man built on a much smaller scale. Nevertheless, Erasmus may be held partly responsible for some of Eliot's flippancies.

Clearly, then, an Elizabethan who had been trained on the Latin *colloquia* would feel no astonishment at finding a good deal of entertainment value, politics, satire and gossip in a language-dialogue. On the contrary he would be inclined to look for these things, with which his Latin dialogues had supplied him, in French or Italian dialogues. He did not find much in many of the modern-language dialogues, hastily put together by hard-pressed refugee schoolmasters, but Florio and Eliot with their wider culture and notable connections did not disappoint him. Thus, although to us it seems strange to find such richness of content in books whose primary purpose (and even Eliot kept that purpose carefully in view) was to teach Italian and French to Englishmen, the Elizabethan student of the "tongues" felt no undue surprise thereat but rather took it as a matter of course that his studies should be spiced with so many fascinating flavours.

Here then are history and tradition leading us to expect that these dialogues by Florio and Eliot might reflect something of their surroundings, of the personalities and interests prevailing in the circle for which they were written. And every line of enquiry pursued in this book has led us to the conclusion that that circle was the one in which Shakespeare was moving. Undoubtedly it is time that the modern-language dialogues of Florio and Eliot should emerge in their true light as documents of great importance to the Shakespearean scholar.

The Countess de Chambrun has always maintained that Florio was already with Southampton when the *Second Fruits* (1591) was written and that the earl's interests and pursuits are reflected in that manual. Although there is still no documentary evidence that Florio was with the earl as early as this she is probably right. Again, Farmer and others used to think that Florio's criticism of the English drama in that book was directed at Shakespeare.[1]

> *H.* The plaies that they plaie in England, are not right comedies.
> *T.* Yet they doo nothing else but plaie euery daye.
> *H.* Yea but they are neither right comedies, nor right tragedies.
> *G.* How would you name them then?
> *H.* Representations of histories, without any decorum.

This idea was later rejected on the ground that Shakespeare had written nothing as early as 1591; but of that we are now by no means so sure. Mr Peter Alexander thinks that he began to write for the stage "some considerable time before 1589".[2] Possibly, therefore, the *Second Fruits* already reflects some of the antagonisms latent in the Southampton circle.

In the case of *Ortho-epia Gallica* there is no already existing tradition to which our case may be attached, for no one has hitherto suspected any connection between this book and Shakespeare.[3] Yet in view of the topical character of the language-dialogues as a class, I do not think that my suggestion that Eliot's poet who has rehearsed "Titius Tragedie" might conceivably be an allusion to Shakespeare himself can be dismissed as entirely fanciful, supported as it is by what I believe to be the connections between *Ortho-epia Gallica* and *Willobie His Avisa*. These are matters which require further careful examination and testing before acceptance. But the way in which we have been able to trace so many of the topical strands in *Love's Labour's Lost* back to these two books of dialogues does

---

[1] See p. 15.   [2] See p. 37.

[3] Eliot's grammar is, however, mentioned in Farmer's essay *On the Learning of Shakespeare*. See D. Nicol Smith, *Eighteenth Century Essays on Shakespeare*, 1903, pp. 211, 344.

tend to confirm the belief that Florio and Eliot were important in Shakespeare's environment during his early years in London.

*   *   *   *

After the consideration of the relationship of our study to Shakespeare's life comes the question of its bearing upon other plays besides the one upon which we have been exclusively concentrating.

There is no space to do more than touch in the briefest and most superficial manner upon the reflections of contemporary persons and contemporary situations which might be discerned in other plays if the key which has fitted the lock of *Love's Labour's Lost* were applied elsewhere. Broadly speaking, the position of those who discern a spirit of pro-Essex faction in some of the plays, particularly the histories, must be, I think, strengthened if the present diagnosis of *Love's Labour's Lost* as a move in the Essex-Raleigh, "artist"-"villanist" sequence is correct. Speaking more in detail, one has only to remember the contrast between the reprobate Sir Toby Belch, who had evidently studied Eliot's French manual, and the prim Malvolio who is so well-versed in the opinions of Pythagoras, to realise that there are possibilities in this direction also. A great many curious indications in *Twelfth Night* might be interpreted as reflections of the Eliot-Florio situation. Again, there come into the mind memories of the foreign accents in *The Merry Wives of Windsor*, or of the alien problems in *Sir Thomas More*. Shades of Eliot and of "Signior Crocodill" may lurk behind Falstaff. If Eliot's contact with Shakespeare is proved, he provides a channel by which knowledge of Rabelais could have reached the dramatist and perhaps have influenced the birth of the fat knight. The anti-Petrarchists of the plays—from Petrucchio to Iago, not forgetting Henry Percy *alias* Harry Hotspur—might be collected and their language compared with that of Pandolpho in the *Second Fruits*. The play in which there is an undoubted quotation from Florio's *Montaigne* contains also Shakespeare's most finished portrait of the man who has devoted himself to the deep search for knowledge and has attained to some foreshadowing of the powers of modern science. Prospero exercised his "arts" in island banishment; other "artists" pursued theirs in the Tower.[1]

Such are a few of the avenues along which this enquiry might be further pursued. And it should be recognised that explorations of this kind are not crude attempts to find "originals" for Shakespearean characters, an unsatisfactory and misleading process. It cannot be too often emphasised that Shakespeare *created* his people, and that they are themselves and no one else. Nevertheless, in our revulsion from misdirected efforts at original-finding we must not go to the other extreme and deny that Shakespeare used his experience, as every imaginative writer must. No creative artist can transcend his age without having grappled with his age. Indeed, his universality is in direct ratio to the firmness with which he has laid hold on the forms under which life presents itself to him in his own experience. The fascination of study of this kind is the opportunity which it gives of placing Shakespeare within the atmosphere of his time and of observing how he confronts its problems.

*　　*　　*　　*

This brings us to our last task. We have tried to place *Love's Labour's Lost* within the atmosphere of the time by showing it to have been a move in a controversy which was then afoot between two rival groups and which turned, in part, upon the question of what is the best way of qualifying as a poet, of achieving full development as a man and—to take it at its highest level—of seeking the

---

[1] An earlier sketch of an "artist" is Owen Glendower, whose scene with Percy is worthy of attention.

light of Truth. One side maintained that all these things were best and most quickly learned in the school of life and of experience of the world. The other side believed that they could only be achieved at the cost of the most rigid intellectual discipline and study, necessitating a certain degree of retirement from the world. We now have to attempt to decide what exactly was Shakespeare's answer to this question which many voices were discussing all around him.

He took the side to which by his temperament and by the nature of his genius he would obviously be inclined— the side of life. Technically he was a "villanist" in this controversy and the villainous taste in humour and innuendo often displayed in this play is, to some extent, a flaunting of the banner under which he marched. In his particular and local aspect, as a man of his time, he falls into place as an Essex-Southampton "villanist" ranged against the Raleigh "artists".

But Shakespeare was far more than a man of his time; he was "for all time", and his contribution to this local controversy entirely transcends all its local patterning and takes on a profound and universal importance. The more the play is studied the more clearly it is seen to be no mere cheap sneer at genuine learning or true scholarship but a psychologically wise warning against the dangers of ill-digested knowledge. Berowne is very far from wishing to exalt stupidity and ignorance. He does not despise knowledge, but he assimilates it thoroughly into his personality. Learning is not something into which he retreats as an escape from life, but something which he carries with him into life.

> Learning is but an adjunct to ourself,
> And where we are our learning likewise is.
> Then, when ourselves we see in ladies' eyes...
> Do we not likewise see our learning there?[1]

[1] IV. iii. 310–14.

This is the secret of what was wrong with the Earl of Northumberland and the "artists" of the "School of Night". They were trying to cultivate a dual nature. They would be noble, profound, and high-souled in the contemplation of knowledge in its height; but in the ordinary contacts of life they could live at an altogether baser and lower level because these were unimportant. This is a false philosophy, for it suggests that matter is in itself evil, and a dangerous psychology for it leads to a disintegrated personality at war within itself. So we might express in our modern jargon what Shakespeare preferred to say in exquisite poetry.

The play is thus a reiteration of a truth which wise men in all ages have always emphasised, that a man must be large enough to absorb and digest his learning, to make it one with himself, to experience it as something which applies to life as he knows it. Those who fail to do this become pedants, persons who, like Holofernes and Armado, think of learning as something external to themselves, a coin or a counter passed from hand to hand to make a glorious show.

> It is not enough to joyne learning and knowledge to the minde, it should be incorporated unto it: it must not be sprinckled, but dyed with it; and if it change not and better her estate (which is imperfect) it were much better to leave it.

So says Montaigne, in Florio's words, and Berowne would endorse the statement.

Learning and experience must then, says Shakespeare, go hand in hand and the one must supplement, not cancel, the other. Be it noted that in spite of the embroidery of "villanist" jokes there is no real villainy—no suggestion of the literary bohemianism or moral laxity which lesser "villanists" possibly condoned—at the heart of this play. Shakespeare's plea for life is a plea for the right kind of love, that rational love between the sexes the search for which was a most noble contribution of the Italian Renaissance[1] towards the civilising of mankind.

One of the lessons which the young men learn in this school of life is a lesson of humility. It is the undigested knowledge of the pedant or the "artist" which leads to pride and which blows him "full of maggot ostentation".[2] The truly wise man is not conceited, because his wisdom is so much a part of him that he is unconscious of it. It was the "superior" air of Raleigh and his friends, their "damnable pride", which contemporaries found so aggravating. *Love's Labour's Lost* is a kind of sermon against spiritual and intellectual pride. At the beginning of the play Berowne and his friends are four rather self-satisfied young men; but the experiences through which they pass are humbling experiences. At the end they are in an altogether more chastened and teachable mood which augurs well for their future development. The excitable Berowne has come to such a pass that a mocking wench can call him a fool with impunity.

> *Berowne.* This jest is dry to me, my gentle sweet.
> Your wit makes wise things foolish: when we greet,
> With eyes best seeing, heaven's fiery eye,
> By light we lose light—your capacity
> Is of that nature that to your huge store
> Wise things seem foolish and rich things but poor.
> *Rosaline.* This proves you wise and rich; for in my eye—
> *Berowne.* I am a fool, and full of poverty.[3]

"I am a fool, and full of poverty." To know this is the beginning of wisdom; and this was what Berowne saw in those eyes where he had thought to see his learning reflected.

---

[1] See L. E. Pearson, *Elizabethan Love Conventions*, 1933, pp. 285 ff., for a discussion of the Italianate conception of rational love in *Love's Labour's Lost*. [2] v. ii. 409.

[3] v. ii. 373–80. The "eye", "light", "rich" allusions are sufficiently obvious. These are lines which give the lie direct to the Earl of Northumberland.

The young men are indeed brought low and they have begun to see the error of their ways, but they are not to be accepted until they have expiated the pride of the flesh and the pride of the intellect in penance. The king is to go for a year into some forlorn and naked heritage, remote from all the pleasures of the world, where he must endure with patience fasts and frosts, hard lodging and thin weeds. A year's trial is also imposed on Longaville and Dumaine. Berowne must spend a twelvemonth in a hospital, using his brilliant gifts in the humble service of unfortunate and unattractive people.

> You shall this twelvemonth term from day to day
> Visit the speechless sick, and still converse
> With groaning wretches; and your task shall be,
> With all the fierce endeavour of your wit,
> To enforce the painéd impotent to smile.[1]

The contrast between these vows and those which were made at the beginning of the play is very striking. If the world is to be renounced, Shakespeare seems to say, it must be from motives of love and pity, not of cold intellectual exclusiveness and pride.

If this is the right interpretation of Shakespeare's answer to Sir Walter Raleigh's "school of atheism",[2] it is singularly like the answer which a good Catholic would have given. The distrust of Copernican astronomers would admit of a similar explanation. And it is also, to my mind, rather curious that a certain parallel—somewhat vague and inconclusive it must be admitted—has been suggested between certain lines in *Love's Labour's Lost* and those in a

---

[1] v. ii. 846–50.
[2] It was Robert Parsons, the Jesuit, who used this expression to describe Raleigh's circle. It has been suggested that Holofernes by his play on "Person" and "Parson" (IV. ii. 85–7) might be alluding to Parsons. See J. Phelps, "Father Parsons in Shakespeare', in *Archiv für das Studium der neueren Sprachen und Literaturen*, 1915, pp. 66–86.

religious poem called *Saint Peters Complaynt* (1595) by Robert Southwell, the Jesuit.[1] Southwell apostrophises the eyes of Christ in these words:

> O sacred eyes! the springs of liuing light,
>   The earthly heauens where angels ioy to dwell...
> Sweet volumes stoard with learning fit for saints,
>   Where bliss'full quires imparadize their minds;
> Wherein eternall studie neuer faints
>   Still finding all, yet seeking all it finds:
> How endlesse is your labyrinth of blisse,
> Where to be lost the sweetest finding is.

This is compared with Berowne on eyes:

> From women's eyes this doctrine I derive:
> They sparkle still the right Promethean fire—
> They are the books, the arts, the academes,
> That show, contain, and nourish all the world.[2]

It has been assumed that this parallel, if it exists, must be due to Southwell copying Shakespeare, but as the Jesuit was in prison from 1592 onwards his chances of having seen *Love's Labour's Lost* performed were small.[3] No one seems to have suggested the possibility that the debt might be the other way round, that Shakespeare might be quoting Southwell, whose poem was published in 1595 and who was executed on 21 February 1595, and that, if so, it is partly of Christian love that Berowne is thinking in his great speech. If there is any echo of Southwell in Berowne the latter seems to me to be the only possible explanation of it and one, moreover, which fits in very aptly with the date now assigned to the play.

It may be objected that *Love's Labour's Lost* is a comedy,

---

[1] *Love's Labour's Lost* in the Cambridge *New Shakespeare*, p. 193; Sir E. K. Chambers, *William Shakespeare*, I, 336; II, 193.

[2] IV. iii. 347–50 and 298–300.

[3] See Mario Praz, "Robert Southwell's *Saint Peter's Complaint* and its Italian Source", *Modern Language Review*, XIX, 273–90.

that the second vows at the end of the play are not introduced in any very serious spirit, and that Berowne's
application of Southwell's words to women's eyes, if true,
is somewhat tasteless. To all of which the answer would be
that a very strict political censorship made the open expression of views of this kind practically impossible, and that
if Shakespeare wished to take this line he could only do so
under a disguise of apparent frivolity.

The greatest care must, however, be taken not to press
this interpretation of Shakespeare's attitude too far. One
must not begin to suspect him of violent partisanship or
intrigue. He was careful to keep out of such things as far
as possible. Also, his friends and enemies cannot be divided
by hard and fast lines of this kind. The Earl of Northumberland and Lord Strange were Catholics; the Earl of
Essex leant, theoretically, towards Puritanism; both Sidney
and he married Walsingham's daughter. It was a part of
the difficulty of the age that the essential issues were all
confused and confounded in this way. If Shakespeare was
at heart Catholic in sympathy his reasons were instinctive
and conservative, rather than political, because he had very
deep spiritual roots in English soil.

But, as has lately been said, whatever his secret thoughts
it is "fairly clear from his familiarity with various portions
of Common Prayer and the Homilies that outwardly he
was a Conformist". If the meaning that I have suggested is
latent in *Love's Labour's Lost*, it is very carefully shrouded.
Indeed it would be possible to argue that Shakespeare is
attacking the so-called "atheists" from the point of view
of Anglican, rather than Catholic, orthodoxy. A recent
study has shown how extensive are the borrowings in
this play from Anglican liturgy and from the Bishops'
Bible.[1] The echoes of the Baptismal service in the king's

---

[1] Richmond Noble, *Shakespeare's Biblical Knowledge*, 1935, pp. 11–
12, 70 ff., 142–7.

speeches and of the Catechism in Berowne's objection to his project,

> For every man with his affects is born,
> Not by might mastred, but by special grace,[1]

would serve as hints of the theological implications of the play's theme. And still more interesting is Mr Noble's suggestion that certain lines recall the controversy between translators of the New Testament as to whether the Greek ἀγάπη should be rendered by the word "charity" or the word "love".

> It is religion to be thus forsworn:
> For charity itself fulfils the law;
> And who can sever love from charity?[2]

The theological aspect of the problems presented by the "School of Night" would be the first to strike Shakespeare's contemporaries and it is certainly in his mind in this play. Difficult though it is to pin him down to any particular creed, one can at least say that one of his positions is Christian. For to the poet's eye, rolling in a fine frenzy from earth to heaven, it seemed that charity was the first essential of illumination.

Bacon, with his face turned towards the future and the new world which was to spring from the new scientific learning, saw "light" as knowledge. Shakespeare doubted lest the new kind of learning, dealing no longer with divine and human values, might loosen the social bonds which unite mankind. Hariot's calculations lead straight on through Newton to the whole modern world, which is so rich in the things of the mind and so poor in the things of the spirit, so ready to trample underfoot those social graces, based on respect and love for the immortal souls of men and women, which alone make life worth living. Perhaps something of this was already visible to one whose eye could pierce to "the prophetic soul of the wide world, dreaming on things to come".

[1] I. i. 151-2.　　　　[2] IV. iii. 360-2.

APPENDICES

I

Extract from Gabriel Harvey's *Pierces Supererogation*, 1593

[Copy used, British Museum, C. 40. d. 9.]

The present consideration of which singularity, occasioneth me to bethinke me of One, that this other day very soberlie commended some extraordinary giftes in Nashe: and when he had grauelie maintayned, that in the resolution of his conscience, he was such a fellowe, as some wayes had few fellowes; at last concluded somewhat more roundly.

Well, my maisters, you may talke your pleasures of Tom Nash; who yet sleepeth secure, not without preiudice to some, that might be more ielous of their name: but assure your selues, if M. Penniles had not bene deepely plunged in a profound exstasie of knauery, M. Pierce had neuer written that famous worke of Supererogation, that now stayneth all the bookes in Paules-churchyard, and setteth both the vniuersites to schoole. Till I see your finest humanitie bestow such a liberall exhibition of conceit, and courage, vpon your neatest wittes; pardon me though I prefer one smart Pamflet o knauery, before ten blundring volumes of the nine Muses. Dreaming, and smoke amount alike: Life is a gaming, a iugling, a scoulding, a lawing, a skirmishing, a warre; a Comedie, a Tragedy: the sturring witt, a quintessence of quicksiluer; and there is noe deade fleshe in affection, or courage. You may discourse of Hermes ascending spirit; of Orpheus enchanting harpe; of Homers diuine furie; of Tyrtæus enraging trumpet; of Pericles bounsinge thunderclaps; of Platos enthusiasticall rauishment; and I wott not what maruelous egges in mooneshine: but a flye for all your flying speculations, when one good fellow with his odd iestes, or one madd knaue with his awke hibber-gibber, is able to putt downe twentye of your smuggest artificiall men, that simper it so nicely, and coylie in their curious pointes. Try, when you meane to be disgraced: & neuer giue me credit, if Sanguine witt putt not Melancholy Arte to bedd. I had almost said, all the figures of Rhetorique must abate me an ace of Pierces Supererogation: and Penniles hath a certayne nimble and climbinge reach of Inuention, as good as a long pole, and a hooke, that neuer fayleth at a pinch. It were vnnaturall, as the sweete Emperour, Marcus Antoninus said, that the fig-tree should euer want iuice. You that purpose with great summes of studdy, & candles to purchase the worshipfull names of Dunses, & Dodipoles, may closely sitt, or sokingly ly at your bookes: but you that intende to be fine companionable gentlemen, smirkinge wittes, and whipsters in the world, betake yee timely to the liuely practis of the minion profession, and enure your Mercuriall fingers to frame semblable workes of Supererogation. Certes other rules are fopperies: and they that will seeke out the Archmistery of the busiest Modernistes, shall find it nether more, nor lesse, than a certayne pragmaticall secret, called Villany, the verie science of sciences, and the Familiar Spirit of Pierces Supererogation. Coosen not your selues with the gay-nothings of children, & schollers: no priuitie of learning, or inspiration of witt, or reuelation of misteryes, or Arte Notory, counteruayleable with Pierces Supererogation: which hauing none of them, hath them all, and can make them all Asses at his pleasure. The Book-woorme was neuer but a pick-goose; it is the Multiplying spirit, not of the Alchimist, but of the villanist, that knocketh the naile one the head, and spurreth cutt farther in a day, then the quickest Artist in a weeke. Whiles other are reading, wryting, conferring, arguing, discoursing, experimenting, platforminge, musing, buzzing, or I know not what: that is the spirrit, that with a woondrous dexterity shapeth exquisite workes, and atchieueth puissant exploites of Supererogation. O my good frends, as ye loue the sweete world, or tender your deare selues, be not vnmindfull what is good for the aduauncemente of your commendable partes. All is nothing without aduauncement. Though my experience be a Cipher in these causes, yet hauing studiously perused the newe Arte-notory, that is, the foresaid Supererogation; and hauing shaken so manie learned asses by the eares, as it were by the hands; I could say no lesse, and might think more.

Something else was vttered the same time by the same Gentleman, aswell concerning the present state of France, which he

termed the most vnchristian kingdome of the most christian kinge;
as touching certaine other newes of I wott not what dependence:
but my minde was running on my halfpeny, and my head so full
of the foresaid round discourse, that my hand was neuer quyet,
vntill I had altered the tytle of this Pamphlet, and newlie christened
it *Pierces Supererogation*: aswell in remembrance of the saide discourse, as in honour of the appropriate vertues of *Pierce* himself; . . .

II

The dedication from George Chapman's
The Shadow of Night, 1594

[Copy used, British Museum, C. 39. d. 62.]

TO MY DEARE AND
MOST VVORTHY FRIEND
MASTER MATHEW ROYDON

It is an exceeding rapture of delight in the deepe search of knowledge, (none knoweth better then thy selfe sweet *Mathew*) that
maketh men manfully indure th'extremes incident to that *Herculean*
labour: from flints must the *Gorgonean* fount be smitten. Men
must be shod by *Mercurie*, girt with *Saturnes* Adamantine sword,
take the shield from Pallas, the helme from *Pluto*, and haue the
eyes of *Græa* (as *Hesiodus* armes *Perseus* against *Medusa*) before
they can cut of the viperous head of benumming ignorance, or
subdue their monstrous affections to most beautifull iudgement.

How then may a man stay his maruailing to see passion-driuen
men, reading but to curtoll a tedious houre, and altogether hide-
bownd with affection to great mens fancies, take vpon them as
killing censures as if they were iudgements Butchers, or as if the
life of truth lay tottering in their verdits.

Now what a supererogation in wit this is, to thinke skil so
mightilie pierst with their loues, that she should prostitutely shew
them her secrets, when she will scarcely be lookt vpon by others
but with invocation, fasting, watching; yea not without hauing

drops of their soules like an heauenly familiar. Why then should our *Intonsi Catones* with their profit-rauisht grauitie esteeme her true fauours such questionlesse vanities, as with what part soeuer thereof they seeme to be something delighted, they queimishlie commende it for a pretie toy. Good Lord how serious and eternall are their Idolatrous platts for riches! no maruaile sure they here do so much good with them. And heauen no doubt will grouill on the earth (as they do) to imbrace them. But I stay this spleene when I remember my good *Mat.* how ioyfully oftentimes you reported vnto me, that most ingenious *Darbie*, deepe searching *Northumberland*, and skill-imbracing *heire of Hunsdon* had most profitably entertained learning in themselues, to the vitall warmth of freezing science, & to the admirable luster of their true Nobilitie, whose high deseruing vertues may cause me hereafter strike that fire out of darknesse, which the brightest Day shall enuie for beautie. I should write more, but my hasting out of towne taketh me from the paper, so preferring thy allowance in this poore and strange trifle, to the pasport of a whole Cittie of others, I rest as resolute as *Seneca*, satisfying my selfe if but a few, if one, or if none like it.

> *By the true admirour of thy vertues*
> *and perfectly vowed friend.*
>
> G. CHAPMAN.

III

Essay by Henry Percy, ninth earl of Northumberland, undated

[Calendared in *Calendar of State Papers, Domestic,* 1603–10, p. 183, where it is assigned to the year 1604, with a query. Reference, S.P. 14, XI, No. 9. Written in a clear secretary hand, with quotations, etc. in italic. 2 ff.]

Be not impatient that yo^w have not the success of my love; I knowe to yo^w the silence in it were nothinge but that yow conceave to me it is somewhat, and that which causeth yo^w to beleve that it is so, is not out of yor owne allowance, but that yo^w fownd I would needs have it so allowed. Yo^w are neerer to me then any, therefore it is veary reasonable that I render yo^w reason and accompte of my pceadinges, least I should demonstrate my self fantasticall in givinge over, or idle in beginninge without iudgement. The platts how disgested, how contrived, yow may remember, the inventions from what conceate they proceeded yo^w did see and weare sorry, my violent passion yow were content to yeeld vnto out of necessitie, because it was otherwise booteles. Those same my best counsells have sit vppon, but in the eand pved addel toyes never hatched for if they had, monsters in my discretion would have bene brought out, my witts wch were then nimble in this kind (for nimblenes groweth by exercise, and exercise from a purpose to obtaine) propownded all manner of consididerations (*sic*) to my vnderstandinge in these vnprofitable courses, so as wadinge into the mistories of this art, I conceaved if shee were yonge and irresolute, kindnes, curtesie, love honorably pfessed, greate care without harshnes was meanes to insinuate a speciall likinge and allowance of advice, tyme, place, and vnbard accesse; If restrained by husbands austerenes, or parents ouer watchfull eyes, then libertie is to be pleaded, bycause it will make her well beleeving in thee. If at libertie then to pleade retyrednes to be most honorable, bycause thy worth only may most be knowen and apparant and not eclipsed with the multitude of virtues dispersed in seu^rall psons. If religiousely disposed, then to remove those feares incident to sinne sometymes by reasons waggishly let slippe, other tymes by reasons more sowndly vttered, and if auriculer confession, pennance, and repentance will not give dispensation, yet the motion of the spirrit may serve for excuse. If she be meerely fettered wth vertue and honno^r, then honorable pastymes and meryments mixt now and then wth a little vnseene swarvinge to the contrary, well and artificially put vppon her and at that tyme vnavoydable, must beguilingly allure her to a little hardines, wch soone wilbe effected, when experience shall teach that they are nothinge, either by not beinge noted, bycause the aspect of the world is apt ever to be cast vppon the most apparent obiects, or else out of self good opinion that will admitt no cleere insighted sight into our owne errors. Stories of tender harts begettinge ends praise worthy may sometymes mollefie a distasted humor to loves pleading. Obsequiousenes, care, passion, and thy virtues magnefied by fitt instruments, must of necessetie breede relentinge: Indeeringe of thyne owne creddit, apparant vigilancy of hers, pswadinge secrecy for thyne owne sake will proffitt. If her affections walke in the laborinth of any others pfections patience and tyme must yeeld the first releef, strattagems well and aptly fitted the second, reiection and carelesnes the last and surest although the most desperate. If a beaten gallant, over passionate is not good for feare of daliance with thee, ouer careles is naught for feare of compassing nothing, and flattery without wonder is not amisse: If shee be glorious and prowde, flattery with wonder is the best. If needie, thy fortune must be present, yet still detayned, otherwise shee will pray vppon thee: bounties forwardnes before it be deserved will cause plonginge. If artifitiall and counterfeytinge the stampe of nature, If letcherous oportunitye, daliance and banquetinge will make the sute shorte, for *Sine Cerere et Baccho friget Venus*. If a Mistris of compownded humors, compownded meanes must be directed. Thus havinge thoroughly considered the wayes in gen⁰all of my pretended happynes, little thinckinge that a *Mathematicall* line beinge lesse then an vntwined thredd could have bene stronger to have stayed me, then eyther fetters or Chaynes. Tumblinge these conceites from corner to corner of my braynes, nothinge resting vndone but how to compownd a mixture fittest to purchase my idle determination, both I and my fancies walked in a Cirkell, the one about the Chamber, the other to the first period of obteininge vntill I grew giddie with thinckinge, and thinckinge gyddelie, made me gyddie in walkinge: weary in this circular maze intisinge these vnstaied companions to a straighter Cabbin, of purpose either to tame them by the rometh,[1] or ease them by certaine bookes that lay scattered amongest the rest: there did I seeke for *Tharcadia*, or bookes of the like subiecte, whereby I might learne to vtter my lethargious passions with there sweete flimflams pleasinge orders: amongest the rest, as a destenie from eternetie prepared to crosse my desires, there lay an owld *Arabian* called *Alhazen*, which wth some anger I angrylie removed, it flying open phapps by reason of a Stationers thred vncutt, yet superstitiouse in my religion that it was the spirrit that directed me by hidden and vncon-

---

[1] Obsolete form of "roomth", used here apparently in the sense of occupation or exercise for the mind. See the *Oxford English Dictionary*.

ceaveable meanes what was good for my purpose, with a discontented eye I beheld it where I pceaved a demonstration of the
colours of the Raynebowe the cause of his arkednes; these thinges
pmised so little for my satisfaction, as in that poynt of booke
openinge doctrine I learned more then half to be a runagate,
bycause that doth ever seeme truestly to be wrought by the
sperrit, that may be best wrested to our wrested opinions; with
a careles hand and a distracted thought not ceasing to shift many
leaves, looking vppon them with earnestnes in apparance, yet
almost marking nothing, I light vppon a place where a figure
seemed somwhat more irreguler then his fellowes, wch caused an
awakinge me out of my muses, and to mark what it imported
with more attention; there did I behold a demonstration declaring
the hight of the aier with no small wonder, bycause it had ever
bene taught me, *Nullum vacuum in rerum natura*. Vnchaining
my mynd from the former conceites to behold the proiect of this
greate pmiser, I studied but still interrupted with the worthes
of my Mistris wch had sealed deeper impressions in my memory:
thus leapinge from the demonstration to my Mistris, and returning
from my Mistris to the demonstration, I gayned so much in the
eand as I vnderstood nether rightly; with patience, (like vnskilfull
Chesplayers with mynd wandring from there games, well vnder-
standing there errors committed thincking to thinke of nothing
else the next tyme) began againe, but ere my eyes had passed
many lines, my thoughtes were againe strayinge, yet at this tyme
my vnderstandinge being somwhat cleered from these obscure
mistes, I pceaved that then probable, which afterwards declared
it self vndenyable; This greate strife of humors continuing, both
beinge yet in equall ballance good in pbabilitie, nether masteringe
the one the other, the one intysinge me to put in execution the
growndes alreadie platted, desire of gnowledge pswadinge me
with earnestnes to consider this latter better: sometymes I thought
if I pursued my Mistris the latter might be obteyned hereafter,
other tymes if I slipt the latter for the present I lost the iewell
of tyme, and exchanged light for darknes, thus taking vp the
booke discardinge my Mistris, other tymes embracinge the conceites of her shadowe I left the booke shutt, againe consideringe
that two or three leaves would satisfie the taske vndertaken,
resolutely I embraced the burden, perused it with attention ioyed

in his witt, allured to looke further into the proofes beinge led from pposition to pposition, vntill I was carryed to the principles of that, and from his principles to the veary principles most simple of knowledge in ge*n*all. Knowledge havinge overwrought the other by the sowndnes of his argumentes, for they remayned demonstrative, my Mistris shaddowes but probable, which afterwards pved meere fallatious. One rule amongest the rest I could not but remember, and that was, *Quæ mutuo congruunt inter se sunt æqualia*; wch being so fitt to examyn whether knowledge or my Mistris in reason showld be predominant over my endevors: Knowledge I fownd spake gravely my Mistris, idelly, it constant, shee fickle, it treated of hidden misteries shee of vulger trifles, it contented ever shee displeased often, it discourst with assurance, shee weakly, it produced out of conclusions ppetuall contentment, shee in conclusion pduced sadnes, for they say *Omne animall post coitum triste.* These examinations declaringe themselves so palpable, as that I feared the imputation of wilfulnes should sooner be attributed to me then true iudgement, since my inwardest conscience would not denye but that the bewties of my Mistris were eclipsed, pceadinge from the perfectest creature vnder the sonne, to the most vggley and deformed of all pfections, not that shee was so amongest women, but in respect of knowledge, for nothinge is faire or fowle simply of it self but in respect. My service thus beinge wholy dedicated to this infinite worthy Mistris, growing cowld towardes my[1] finite Mistris, and fearinge least some not rightly conceavinge of both, might censure this vnconstancy a fault, necessarie it was to the avoydinge of an imputed condemnation, to fortefie this acte by stronge reasons since the deede doth argue his owne goodnes; and strengthninge the cause by vnfowldinge the inconveniencies followinge the one and the benifitts in beinge vassall to the other, I must not be ignorant that in the first there is, myndes disquiet, attendant servitude, flatteringe observance, losse of tyme, passion without reason, observinge base creatures, torture of iealowsie, allowance of tryfles, toyle of body, hazard of pson, decrease of health, losse of reputation, prodigall expence, slackinge of good actions, scornefull disgraces, feare of future reward. In the other myndes quiet, sowles felicitie, resolu-

---

[1] The copyist wrote "his" first here, and corrected it to "my".

tion of futur state, wonderinge at nothinge, Inseeinge into all, iudiciall above ordenary, free from passions, of nothinge fearefull, in all thinges happie, in nothinge vnfortunate or overioyinge, good deedes in aboundance, honored of the most, embracing goodnes for goodnes sake. But least I showld open my humor to be over enclyning to a *Cynicall* disposition, and that knowledge could not be enterteynd w^thout the losse of a Mistris, I must conclude that to enioye a Mistris together with learninge is possible, but to gaine a Mistris with longe sute, mutch passion, and many delaies, and follow knowledge in his hight is impossible.

[Contemporary endorsement in a different hand to the text] My lo. of Northumb.

[Modern pencil endorsements] 1605, 1604? James I? On the entertainment of a Mistress being inconsistent with the pursuit of Learning.

INDEX